ALSO BY WHITNEY CASARES, MD, MPH, FAAP

The New Baby Blueprint: Caring for You and Your Little One

MORE FROM THE AMERICAN ACADEMY OF PEDIATRICS

Achieving a Healthy Weight for Your Child: An Action Plan for Families

ADHD: What Every Parent Needs to Know

Autism Spectrum Disorder: What Every Parent Needs to Know

Baby and Toddler Basics: Expert Answers to Parents' Top 150 Questions

Building Resilience in Children and Teens: Giving Kids Roots and Wings

Caring for Your Adopted Child: An Essential Guide for Parents

Caring for Your Baby and Young Child: Birth to Age 5*

Caring for Your School-Age Child: Ages 5–12

Co-parenting Through Separation and Divorce: Putting Your Children First

Family Fit Plan: A 30-Day Wellness Transformation

Heading Home With Your Newborn: From Birth to Reality

My Child Is Sick! Expert Advice for Managing Common Illnesses and Injuries

Parenting Through Puberty: Mood Swings, Acne, and Growing Pains

The Picky Eater Project: 6 Weeks to Happier, Healthier Family Mealtimes

Protecting Your Child's Health: Expert Answers to Urgent Environmental Questions

Quirky Kids: Understanding and Supporting Your Child With Developmental Differences

Raising an Organized Child: 5 Steps to Boost Independence, Ease Frustration,
and Promote Confidence

Raising Kids to Thrive: Balancing Love With Expectations and Protection With Trust

Retro Baby: Cut Back on All the Gear and Boost Your Baby's Development With More
Than 100 Time-tested Activities

Retro Toddler: More Than 100 Old-School Activities to Boost Development
Your Baby's First Year*

**For additional parenting resources, visit the HealthyChildren bookstore
at https://shop.aap.org/for-parents.**

healthy children.org
Powered by pediatricians. Trusted by parents.

*This book is also available in Spanish.

The Working Mom Blueprint

Winning at Parenting Without Losing Yourself

WHITNEY CASARES,
MD, MPH, FAAP

American Academy of Pediatrics
DEDICATED TO THE HEALTH OF ALL CHILDREN®

AMERICAN ACADEMY OF PEDIATRICS PUBLISHING STAFF

Mary Lou White, *Chief Product and Services Officer/SVP, Membership, Marketing, and Publishing*
Mark Grimes, *Vice President, Publishing*
Holly Kaminski, *Editor, Consumer Publishing*
Jason Crase, *Senior Manager, Production and Editorial Services*
Shannan Martin, *Production Manager, Consumer Publications*
Peg Mulcahy, *Manager, Art Direction and Production*
Sara Hoerdeman, *Marketing Manager, Consumer Products*

Published by the American Academy of Pediatrics
345 Park Blvd
Itasca, IL 60143
Telephone: 630/626-6000   Facsimile: 847/434-8000
www.aap.org

The American Academy of Pediatrics is an organization of 67,000 primary care pediatricians, pediatric medical subspecialists, and pediatric surgical specialists dedicated to the health, safety, and well-being of all infants, children, adolescents, and young adults.

The information contained in this publication should not be used as a substitute for the medical care and advice of your pediatrician. There may be variations in treatment that your pediatrician may recommend based on individual facts and circumstances.

Statements and opinions expressed are those of the author and not necessarily those of the American Academy of Pediatrics.

Any websites, brand names, products, or manufacturers are mentioned for informational and identification purposes only and do not imply an endorsement by the American Academy of Pediatrics (AAP). The AAP is not responsible for the content of external resources. Information was current at the time of publication.

The persons whose photographs are depicted in this publication are professional models. They have no relation to the issues discussed. Any characters they are portraying are fictional.

The publishers have made every effort to trace the copyright holders for borrowed materials. If they have inadvertently overlooked any, they will be pleased to make the necessary arrangements at the first opportunity.

This publication has been developed by the American Academy of Pediatrics. The contributors are expert authorities in the field of pediatrics. No commercial involvement of any kind has been solicited or accepted in the development of the content of this publication. Disclosure: Dr Casares reports consultant relationships with Evivo (Evolve Biosystems) and Gerber.

Every effort is made to keep *The Working Mom Blueprint: Winning at Parenting Without Losing Yourself* consistent with the most recent advice and information available from the American Academy of Pediatrics.

Special discounts are available for bulk purchases of this publication. Email Special Sales at nationalaccounts@aap.org for more information.

Printed in the United States of America
9-464/0321   1 2 3 4 5 6 7 8 9 10

CB0124
ISBN: 978-1-61002-486-0
eBook: 978-1-61002-489-1
EPUB: 978-1-61002-487-7
Kindle: 978-1-61002-488-4

Cover and publication design by Peg Mulcahy
Library of Congress Control Number: 2020937638

Praise for Books by Dr Whitney Casares

The Working Mom Blueprint

Dr Casares' vital message in this warmly reassuring, deeply empathetic book is that when you practice better self-care, you will take better care of everyone—and everything—else. It's filled with practical, actionable tools and tips that even the most sleep-deprived, bleary-eyed working mother can follow.

—Jancee Dunn, author of *How Not to Hate Your Husband After Kids*

Children thrive when their parents love them without condition…and feel whole themselves. Parenting is the hardest and most important job we have. Sacrifice isn't the answer. Perfection is not an option. Good parenting is about caring beyond measure while wisely guiding our children in their journey towards adulthood. Being satisfied with our lives outside of parenting is precisely what gives us the strength to parent well. Dr Casares "gets real" in *The Working Mom Blueprint* and hits it out of the park! This book is exactly what modern parents need to get to that beautiful balanced space where they can love with every bit of their energy precisely because their tanks are filled in other areas of their lives.

—Kenneth R. Ginsburg, MD, MS Ed, FAAP, author of *Building Resilience in Children and Teens* and *Raising Kids to Thrive* and director of the Center for Parent and Teen Communication at the Children's Hospital of Philadelphia

As a working pediatrician-mom of 4 teenagers, I've experienced the "seasons" Dr Casares describes in *The Working Mom Blueprint*. She sagely advises parents to give ourselves grace and to recognize "This life is all about choices…trade-offs and benefits." Dr Casares shares timely and topical advice, empowering parents to not only prioritize what is truly important but also to serve as role models for our children to continue tilting the needle towards greater gender equity in both our households and our workplaces.

—Shelly Vaziri Flais, MD, FAAP, pediatrician and author of *Raising Twins*, editor in chief of *Caring for Your School-Age Child*, coeditor of *The Big Book of Symptoms*, and assistant professor of clinical pediatrics at Northwestern University Feinberg School of Medicine

As working moms, the impenetrable feeling that because we can do anything means we should do "everything" creates exhaustion. Dr Casares conveys a reassuring perspective that not only can we release the pressure but that we must, and walks the reader through a path that feels practical, believable, kind, and wise.

—Amy Stoeber, PhD, licensed psychologist and creator of the courses *The Art of Imperfect Parenting* and *The Kids Will Be OK*

The New Baby Blueprint

They say motherhood doesn't come with a manual, but *The New Baby Blueprint*, brought to you by the American Academy of Pediatrics, comes pretty close.... [A] relatable mix of humor and practical advice.
　—Ashlee Neuman, *The Bump*

Casares...knows both personally and professionally the struggles parents face in the first few months of their child's life....A quick read with a parent-friendly format, this will be especially helpful for new parents.
　—*Library Journal*

Dr Casares has written a parenting manual that helps new and experienced caregivers of infants not just survive but thrive. Writing in an often humorous conversational style, Dr Casares comes across not only as a knowledgeable expert on newborn parenting but also as a life coach whose advice is sound, reassuring, evidence based, and inspirational!
　—Lewis First, MD, MS, FAAP, professor and chair, Department of Pediatrics, University of Vermont Larner College of Medicine; chief of pediatrics, University of Vermont Children's Hospital; and editor in chief, *Pediatrics*

In this internet age of numerous "experts" giving advice on parenting, Dr Casares, a skilled pediatrician and mother, distills down volumes of information into a single, easy-to-read guide. Her book is honest and practical—a fresh focus on the mother's needs as well as those of the infant. Her candidness about her own struggles with bringing her babies home, combined with her work with countless new mothers in her practice, informs this modern blueprint for the well-being of the professional mother and her family.
　—Nicole Cirino, MD, reproductive psychiatrist; director, Women's Mental Health Program, Oregon Health & Science University (OHSU) Center for Women's Health; and professor of obstetrics and gynecology and of psychiatry, OHSU

A wonderful, practical resource! With both the good sense of a mom who's "been there, done that" and the seasoned experience of a pediatrician who's helped hundreds of moms navigate the same journey, Dr Casares offers wise guidance and practical tips to parents of newborns. Easy to read, it strikes the right balance between an overall approach to parenting and practical advice on the nitty-gritty details. It's like having coffee with a best friend who, by the way, just happens to be an expert on all things related to new babies and new moms. I can't imagine a better baby shower gift.
　—Janelle Aby, MD, FAAP, author of *The Newborn Book: Significance of Physical Findings in the Neonate* and clinical professor of pediatrics at Stanford University School of Medicine

Pediatricians often get emails, texts, and calls from friends seeking parenting advice from someone with a pediatric medical background. Dr Casares wrote a book that meets this need! She blends practical parenting tips and medical knowledge in this fresh and fun perspective on parenting. It's a great read for any parent who is interested in the pediatrician-mom perspective!
—Lauren Rose, MD, FAAP, newborn and pediatric hospitalist

Dr Casares shares her expertise on newborns from her professional roles as pediatrician and mom in a funny, practical, and down-to-earth manner. Her book provides the most practical advice for new moms that I have read…from preparing for the birth of the child to managing expectations of new moms and sharing her own personal experiences to giving parents-to-be all they need to know but were never told about having a baby. New moms everywhere will find this guide to being a parent invaluable and refer to it again and again.
—Deborah Rumsey, executive director, Children's Health Alliance

Equity, Diversity, and Inclusion Statement

The American Academy of Pediatrics is committed to principles of equity, diversity, and inclusion in its publishing program. Editorial boards, author selections, and author transitions (publication succession plans) are designed to include diverse voices that reflect society as a whole. Editor and author teams are encouraged to actively seek out diverse authors and reviewers at all stages of the editorial process. Publishing staff are committed to promoting equity, diversity, and inclusion in all aspects of publication writing, review, and production.

Contents

Preface

It should have been a perfect day; however, it wasn't. It was summer 2020, the worst summer ever—aka, coronavirus disease 2019 (COVID-19) summer. My friend Stephanie and I had been planning for it for a month. The July sun was shining and our kids were splashing happily in the lake. We'd hiked down with a full bag of granola bars and peanut butter and jelly sandwiches for the littles, packing canned wine, salami, and fancy cheese for the 2 of us. We finally had a break to do something fun. We were warm and sandy and… stressed. And although we were making the best of it—on this particular outing we were sitting 6 feet apart with separate, sanitized packages of food and a whole lot of yelling, "Keep a distance! Remember, give space!" to our children— we both felt like we were barely making it in most ways.

Front and center on both of our minds was the looming school year ahead. What were we going to do? How was this going to work? Stephanie had been a staff physical therapist for a local company for the past 10 years, trying hard to prove herself professionally while honoring the needs of her 3 girls and herself. Steadily, slowly, she built a specialty in women's pelvic floor physical therapy to differentiate herself amongst her colleagues, hoping to earn a director role, but now that seemed like the least of her worries. Suddenly, it was like life—especially work life—was completely in limbo, like some in-between, never-ending twilight zone.

The school options were overwhelming, though she and I both knew we were lucky to even have options. Distance learning, pods, outdoor school, in-person classes…suddenly, choices we never thought we'd consider (and knew we couldn't afford) were in the running, though none of them seemed ideal. And even though we were trying to plan in concrete terms, we didn't have enough specific information for half of the options we considered to add them or cross them off the list.

For hours we went back and forth about the pros and cons, trying to consider the unique needs of our children, exhausted at the end but not any closer to feeling settled about our plans. Stephanie was contemplating sending her children to in-person public school (an option for her district but not mine). Should we try to find a private option? What about child care for the youngest? Was that safe? Would it stay open? What would happen if they got sick from a non-COVID illness? Wouldn't that mean we'd be out of work for several weeks caring for them anyway? How would our decisions affect their mental health? How were we going to pay for all of this? These were the same questions I'd been advising my patients, and as I learned myself, each individual family has its own set of physical health and mental health risk factors, financial considerations, and schedule needs. There is no one-size-fits-all answer to the question: what should I do about child care and school during the COVID-19 pandemic?

Our husbands seemed less worried that day when we filled them in on our conversation and what options we came up with. Sure, they had their own stressors in general. They were both physical therapists too, and seeing patients day in and day out, sanitizing, masking up over and over, was a struggle, but their concern from the get-go about how we would handle work and home and kids was not on our level. They cared about the well-being and safety of their kids, but they did not feel wholly responsible for ensuring it as working dads in the same way we did as working moms. Like had been true time and time before in our motherhood experiences, we bore the brunt of these decisions.

COVID-19 is a major stress for parents globally. Over and over again in my pediatrics clinic, parents ask me for advice about how to handle it. "When can our new baby's grandparents come and visit?" "Is it safe to go to the grocery store?" "Will my 3-year-old's social development be stunted if he can't attend preschool this year?" The questions are weighing heavily on everyone.

Moms and dads alike are, understandably, scared about how to protect their children from the virus and how to prevent its spread in their communities. It is mothers, though, that comment most often about the way COVID affects their home and work lives and their ability to balance the two. As working moms have learned through the pandemic that child care can be unpredictable or unreliable. We've also reconfirmed that be it a teacher strike, snow days, or some crisis we haven't yet imagined, the burden of disrupted child care falls disproportionately on mothers (as does most everything else). Not having a solid, reliable plan can make families feel unsettled.

"I took a COVID-19 leave of absence," mom after mom tells me over video chat or in their car as I examine their sick kids. "I didn't have a choice. If I wanted my kids to be in public school this year, it meant I had to be their full-time teacher. At the same time, I need my job so we can pay the bills. So, here we are, with me on my Zoom calls and my kids on theirs. All day long I juggle their full schedules at the exact same time I juggle mine. I'm a terrible teacher, and now I'm barely hanging in there at work. It's going about as well as you can expect."

As stressful as it is, there are ways to make working from home all day, every day, with young kids around as successful as possible (see Chapter 11 for specific tips and solutions), but no mom would wish that level of tension on herself long-term if offered an alternative. The problem is, for many of us, there are no alternatives right now. These moms, like you and me, are doing the best they can day in and day out to manage it all. Being a working mom, even in "normal" times, is stressful enough. But now? Now the stress is sometimes just too much.

I remember in early April 2020 hiding in a closet from my 2 girls in the middle of the day. While I thought a few months prior I'd be enjoying looking forward to spring break and carrying out my regular drop-off routine for school, we were all home—cramped, shocked, and miserable. The laundry was piling up, the kids were getting cranky, and I was definitely on edge. Child care and school were canceled, and my office was closed to most in-person appointments, but the work had to go on. So, there I was, in a closet, trying hard to concentrate on finishing urgent patient notes and attending emergency administrative meetings while my kids wondered where I'd disappeared to. It only took about 20 minutes before I heard them calling my name.

"Mom?!?!! We need you! She's bugging me…and I don't want that movie!"

I muted myself, turned my webcam off, and tried to get them settled while I half-listened to the conversation going on without me on the computer. My kids were upset, my business partners didn't look happy, and I was definitely feeling conflicted. I wasn't a full parent or a full employee in that moment—caught in the middle as I tried to keep all the balls in the air.

COVID-19 has made our juggling act as moms even more complicated and obvious, but, in the end, it showed just how much we all take on, in times of crisis but also in non-pandemic times. Back in 2019, when life was hectic and kids were overscheduled, I spent a lot of hours in my pediatrics clinic counseling parents on the value of paring down their children's extracurricular activities, volunteer commitments, and school obligations—and their own. 2020 changed all that, even for those of us with young kids. There was suddenly no pressure anymore to sign up for piano lessons. The weekend birthday parties were all canceled. No one needed me to come to an in-person parent-teacher conference at 7:30 pm, thank goodness.

Quarantine also had one other benefit: togetherness—a shiny diamond in a dark coal mine. We took more time on Saturday mornings to make blueberry pancakes and sausage because there was nothing else to do. We went together on long walks because there just weren't many other options. We read more. You could feel the simplicity, the exhale we were taking from our prior day-to-day. We had a fresh slate—a new, totally bizarre opportunity to flip the script on the hectic way we all lived pre-COVID.

Our weekend and afternoon schedules were lighter, but, given the circumstances of our free time, the mood was palpably heavier throughout the week. This is a time of grief in so many ways for adults and children alike. Overnight our kids' worlds were flipped upside down. Everything was suddenly a no—no school, no gymnastics, no playdates, no playgrounds. No, no, no. Closed, canceled, coronavirus. With togetherness came *too much* togetherness, a stifling, overcrowding from sharing space hour after hour, day after day. My sensitive firstborn, who needs structure and routine to mitigate her anxiety symptoms, wouldn't even speak the word *coronavirus* (or let us speak it, for that matter) for 3 whole months. Like so many other kids I've worked with this during the pandemic, she regressed and acted out.

Moms continue to come to my office over and over feeling completely overwhelmed, especially those with children with high needs. It's hard enough as adults to understand our own fears, frustrations, and disappointments in a pandemic. As a child, when the world turns on its head, it's understandably not just jarring but, for some, can be traumatic.

As working moms, our worlds were rocked too, not only because we were unexpectedly reeling ourselves but because we carry the emotional well-being of our entire families. What a moment to remind ourselves of the collaborative problem-solving philosophy that kids do the best they can when they can, and so do parents, honing in on taking care emotionally of our young children with evidence-based parenting strategies, empathy, and grace (see Chapter 8 for more on supporting the physical and emotional health of toddler and elementary school kids). What an opportunity to develop real resilience by leaning into our emotions instead of pretending everything's alright.

One well-meaning administrator at my pediatric office attempted to coach us medical professionals in a virtual meeting when we opened back up for well visits after our initial lockdown.

"Remember, you set the tone. Encourage the families and be positive."

One of our staff psychologists stopped her in her tracks.

"I so appreciate what you're trying to say. It's good to be encouraging, but it's also OK not to be OK, and we need to tell parents that. *That's* what parents need to hear right now."

Mama, that's what I want to tell you. It's what I want you to remember. You are allowed to not be OK in this moment. You're allowed to be worried, to feel like you're failing, to feel sometimes like it's just too hard. It's OK to feel like you are living in an alternate universe because you *are* living in an alternate, totally crazy, science-fictional universe, one that can leave you lonely and discouraged most days. It makes sense when you feel flooded with emotions and exhausted by how long this is all taking. After all, back in March 2020, we thought we'd just buckle down for 6 to 8 weeks and be back to business as usual. Clearly, things have not turned out that way, and we now realize we're in a marathon, not a sprint.

I want to tell you that you are not alone in all this. You could fill coliseum after coliseum with moms exactly like you, experiencing the same feelings and struggles, trying to teach their second graders the same phonics, trying not to get video calls bombed by their 9-month-olds' crying. Recognizing our common humanity helps us through hard times, throughout our working mom lives, but especially now.

At the same time, you need to know that, even when we're feeling numb and beaten down by external forces we cannot control ourselves, we *can* control how we respond to them. Now is not a time to crumble and fall but a time to rise up, not with the kind of brute strength, grit your teeth, and hang on by your fingernails approach we're accustomed to adopting as moms when life gets complicated, but with a more sustainable, grounded methodology. If we want to pivot and adapt to the COVID-19 world we're living in we, ironically, have to start doing the things we should have been doing before we ever heard the words "socially distanced."

● **Constantly remind ourselves about what matters most to us in life and what we want out of it.**
It may seem like your hopes and dreams for your life and for your loved ones' lives are now completely out of reach. All our travel plans are off the table; our career advancement opportunities are stymied—sometimes it's hard enough just to get from breakfast to bedtime. How can we look to the future with any kind of confidence? But having a centered vision of how we want our lives to look in 5 to 10 years and a set of priorities we live by (see Chapter 3 for more) is, in fact, exactly what we need to keep hope alive when the days are long and the future looks far away.

● **Adopt a loyal commitment to making space for ourselves.**
Only when we take care of our own physical and social-emotional health can we fully take care of others, especially in times of crisis. The most joyful and centered moms, crisis or no crisis, make concrete plans to attend to their own needs and to intentionally care for themselves in real, practical ways. You still need time to be you, *just you*, throughout the week so you can reconnect to your centered vision but also so you can reconnect to yourself as an individual who is separate from your role as a mom, partner, professional, or friend. COVID-19 doesn't diminish that need; it amplifies it.

Putting our deepest needs first actually allows us to operate from a place of presence and calm, instead of reactivity. Never is this truer that when we have a multitude of outside stressors (like a rapidly spreading virus ruining each and every part of our lives). In Chapter 5 we talk about how to develop a daily ritual, weekly routine, and lifelong commitment that honors ourselves.

When there's a worldwide pandemic (or even when we're going through challenging stages in our children's lives, like the newborn period, the "terrible 2s," or a hard moment with a teenager) we need even more time and space to cultivate joy than we otherwise would. That means when there is a good song playing in the car, we stop, close our eyes, and allow ourselves to just be in the moment with it. When our children want to snuggle for a little longer, we move closer to them on the couch. When there are options to automate and delegate chores and tasks, we pass them off or eliminate them (see Chapter 11 for how to do it). When there are times to eat good food and sit around with your family, we make time for it.

I had a good reminder on this one the other night. My husband couldn't help but stare at me as I shoveled cold rotisserie chicken leftovers into my mouth for a makeshift dinner after a late work meeting.

"Is that even good?" he asked.

"No, not really," I answered back as I choked down the dry meat.

"For goodness sake," he said. "Order some Indian food already. There aren't a lot of pleasures in life right now, but that one's still there."

● **Treat ourselves like we would treat our very best friend on her hardest day.**
As moms, it's easy to treat ourselves harshly when we mess up—and mama, you're in very good company if you've been messing up a lot more these days. Emotions are

running high, our kids have no normalcy, we haven't had a date night in months; it makes sense. We're all too good at criticizing ourselves when we feel like we're failing in one area of life or another—or in all the areas.

The most successful parents learn to emotion-coach our kids, acknowledging and helping them identify their feelings, validating their emotions, and then helping them to problem solve when they get upset. We can't forget to do the same for ourselves too (see Chapter 8 for more on how to help your kids when they're having a tough time and how to regulate your own emotions when you're triggered).

● **Connect with those in our support networks, even if we have to be creative about it.**
Adopting an intention around the way we want to show up for ourselves and for our children during the pandemic is crucial, but doing it alongside others you respect and love is also critical in times like these. You still need a village. Look at your own circle and reach out in a way that honors your particular circumstances. Host a virtual happy hour with your besties, call your mom, invest in creating a strong foundation with your partner (see Chapter 10 for more). The chance to connect, talk, and laugh—sharing in the good moments and the really hard ones—is powerful and encouraging.

● **Learn to trust our instincts—and to remember other struggles we've made it through.**
You are an amazing mom even if, during this pandemic, you don't feel like it at all. You can trust yourself to make the right decisions for you and your family. Think back on the times you weren't exactly sure what to do with your 6-week-old's diaper rash, or when you had no clue how to fix your toddler's thumb-sucking issue. What did you do? You read about it, you relied on trusted experts like your child's pediatrician, but you also relied on your

own intuition. The more you listen to your gut instincts, the more confident your parenting and your sense of self. That's true any day, any year, but it's never been truer than right now.

☙☙☙☙

There aren't many silver linings to speak of in this tumultuous, unsettling time. Financial strain, suboptimal learning environments, social isolation, emotional turmoil, a professional mom regression—I can't wait for relief from all of that. I do believe, though, that we have a unique opportunity right now to make changes and commitments about the way we live our lives that can, if we let them, have a profound effect long after this pandemic is over. Let's not skip too quickly over that lesson.

With COVID-19, we all are facing some kind of crisis or another—at the workplace, at home, in the balance of both—and we each have our own stories. Those stories are unique and the situations are highly individualized, but the steps to handle times of crisis with grace, no matter what the cause or issue, are universal. Trust yourself and take care of yourself. Get an outside set of ears and eyes (or some virtual hugs) when you need them. Give yourself and your family permission to feel deeply and to make mistakes. Take a deep breath and remember this too shall pass. There is joy on the other side, mama, and, I promise, there is even joy here now.

You've got this.

Acknowledgments

Thank you to the amazing women (and men) who made this work complete. Thanks to Caroline Ghiossi, my best research and idea partner; to Christie Artis, who taught me how to think more clearly about how to find what matters; to Lisa McLaughlin, my oldest childhood friend and my fellow dreamer; to Maegan Megginson and Kristen Genzano, who help me see the truth about myself and my relationships; to Jennifer Bissig, Ann Marie Miner, Jennifer Mueller, Amanda Vaughn, Hope Cochran, Michelle Combs, and Kristin Valerius, who gave their time providing their professional insights and personal experiences; to Lauren Edmonds at Evernew Photography, who provided the Modern Mommy Doc website photography; to my Modern Mommy Doc team: Nichole Maggio, Gina Czupryna, Devon Garner, Elizabeth Exline, and Ashley Harrison; to the talented Barbara Teszler at Teszler PR, Inc; to the American Academy of Pediatrics (AAP) Publishing team, including Barrett Winston and my editor, Holly Kaminski; to my AAP peer reviewers: Shelly Vaziri Flais, MD, FAAP, Committee on Nutrition, Council on Early Childhood, and Section on Breastfeeding; to my own mom, who taught me that being a working mother is the best job out there; and to my husband, who is my parenting teammate and my heart's home.

Why a Book for Working Moms?

*I*t's not looking good for my children's gold star status on the behavior board today. One of my children is at the indoor play gym posturing for her position in line for the slide. The other is grabbing her sister's toy out of her hands, seemingly oblivious to the shrieks of offense and horror coming from her sibling. I'm trying to stay focused on managing their behavior as an urgent text comes through from my office, dividing my attention and making my attempts at manhandling 2 rascals much more difficult. I've been up since 5:30 am, when I woke on my third alarm in time to make it to an exercise class and get some "me" time in. It's technically my day off today, but it sure feels like my day on.

That's the story I hear day in and day out as I connect with working moms in my pediatrics practice, and it's how I'm tempted to feel too. Raising children is hard. So is working full time, taking care of a household, maintaining a thriving romantic relationship with a partner, and taking care of yourself. No amount of education or expertise makes this thing called modern motherhood any less challenging, even if you're a Stanford-trained pediatrician and run a website on the topic on the side. Just like the next mom, I have a lot to juggle, and I'm a work in progress as I try to manage it with grace and perspective. I continue to move toward equity with my partner at home. I do my absolute best at work. I'm committed to making sure my kids feel loved and cared for while

I'm figuring out ways to stay sane and whole myself. It's all a dance, and, sometimes, it's a clumsy, off-rhythm one at best.

Moms who read my first book, *The New Baby Blueprint: Caring for You and Your Little One*, said they were most inspired by the advice I gave on coping with the transition to motherhood. When I sat down to figure out what wisdom I wanted to impart in this book, I knew the advice I gave about coping well would also be the most critical here. I realized writing about life beyond the initial postpartum period would be more challenging because it's so much more complicated. I also realized that I often still felt pretty unwise myself, even though I give parenting advice all day in clinic and have built a career and community via Modern Mommy Doc, as I muddle through motherhood. How do you expertly share tips and tricks for balancing life and work when you don't do it perfectly yourself?

That's when I came to my truth: I've become an expert on helping moms in the early years because I myself learned to give up on mothering perfection a long time ago. I've seen way too many modern moms who are, in large part, struggling and failing *because* they're trying to do it all, *all the time*. I've decided it's not worth it. I've honed in on the true, freeing message we actually need: our constant yearning for perfect balance is exactly what's leading us astray—stealing our joy and ruining modern motherhood. And that's why I wrote this book—because we don't need another "5 steps to instant success" kind of working mommy manual—the kind that focuses only on tactical strategies for doing *more*. We do need a philosophically based "take a step back so we can get some perspective" kind of guide—the kind that allows us to do *less* and reach a deeper level of joy and contentment at our jobs and at home with our family.

Everyone knows that being a mom itself is tough and that working moms shoulder a unique kind of stress. In homes with 2 working parents, moms almost always take on the majority of the household workload, even if both parents work full time. In single-parent homes, mothers or fathers are struggling to handle everything alone. In 2-home families, the coordination and collaboration create an extra layer of chaos. Working moms have full-time expectations at work plus full-time expectations at home plus societal pressures to be perfect. Oh, yeah, and how can you forget the mommy guilt, all while juggling these things and making everyone happy? We're pulled too thin, stretched too far. We're overloaded, but it feels like, even though something has got to give, everything will fall apart if anything does.

Sociologist Caitlyn Collins, author of *Making Motherhood Work: How Women Manage Careers and Caregiving*, studied parenting paradigms in 4 wealthy Western countries.

> Across the countries where I conducted interviews, one desire remained constant among mothers. Women wanted to feel that they were able to combine paid employment and child-rearing in a way that seemed equitable and didn't disadvantage them at home or at work. The United States is an outlier among Western industrialized countries for its lack of support for working mothers.

Collins found that American moms seem to have it the worst when it comes to trying to balance conflicts between work and family and that they see it all as their fault—as a personal problem—when really structural problems and cultural norms are to blame.

> I want American moms to stop blaming themselves. I want American mothers to stop thinking that somehow their conflict is their own fault, and that if they tried a little harder, got a new schedule, woke up a little earlier every morning, using the right planner or the right app, that they could somehow figure out the key to managing their stress. That's just not the case.

Turns out, working harder at mothering, "doing it all," is overrated and exhausting. It burns us out, making us anxious, frazzled, and resentful.

That's why this book is not going to tell you how to do it all. It won't offer 3-step solutions to every working motherhood problem, not because the problems don't exist or because they're not worth solving, but because some of them won't ever be settled until society adapts and evolves. This book is not going to teach you how to balance your life perfectly. You'll find practical help for simplifying and for laying a foundation of efficiency, but it won't make you a superhero, able to do anything and everything in your 24-hour day. In fact, here's the most important message I want you to take away after you get to the very last page: *You can't do everything if you want to do anything well.* You'll have to accept that there are trade-offs and benefits to every decision that you make and you'll have to make some tough decisions as a working mom about your priorities if you want to actually enjoy anything. If you do, the sky is the limit on the joy-o-meter.

This book is also not going to teach you how to care for yourself perfectly as you mother. Self-care is important, but we miss the point when we approach self-care like it exists in a vacuum for mothers or like it is the be-all and end-all. It doesn't, and it isn't. Self-care is important but requires prioritizing and compromising when you have kids. It requires overcoming guilt and, often, getting a reluctant partner on board. Successful self-care has to work for you and your budget, which may change, depending on the season of your life. Self-care is not about checking off a box or about using a certain formula. It's about returning to yourself, about finding joy.

Finally, this book is not going to teach you solely how to win at work. We won't talk about how to fight for the corner office, about how to climb the corporate ladder, or about how to "really make it," because I strongly believe that "making it" doesn't necessarily mean being single-minded or being top dog in a corporation. It can include professional achievement, but it doesn't have to. Truly successful modern working moms know that winning at work matters but that winning at parenting matters too (and that, if they lose themselves in the process, it was all for nothing). Their mission is complicated; their struggle is complex. Working moms want to find balance; they want to find long-term contentment; and, above all, they want to promote the social-emotional health of their kids and of themselves.

That's what you'll learn in *The Working Mom Blueprint: Winning at Parenting Without Losing Yourself:* how to approach motherhood with perspective and intention, how to make room for the most important things in your life—the things that make you *you,* for the things that give you joy, and how to balance it all. You'll find real stories from real moms— moms who are flawed but not failing, whose tips and tricks for keeping it all together will work 99% of the time but who also recognize that some days are total lost causes.

This book is deeply personal to me and to the other working moms who contributed to it. There are stories no one else has heard, Confessions From Working Moms; moms I interviewed sobbed through as they recalled them to me. They shared their journeys so you could either follow suit or learn from their mistakes. You'll find brutal honesty and real hope—hope in the reality that being a working mom is hard but worth it, that you are an amazing parent—not in spite of the fact you work but because you do. We'll find hope that, as a working mom, you *can win at parenting without losing yourself.*

Chapter 1

Doing Away With Single-minded Grit

If you're offered a seat on a rocket ship,
don't ask what seat! Just get on.

—*Sheryl Sandberg*

CONFESSIONS FROM WORKING MOMS: Katie is a human resources executive. She rose quickly in the ranks through hard work and a heavy focus on her career. She is celebrated by her peers and has upward mobility. She is so capable and smart that she can do anything she sets her mind to. Now that she has had her second child, though, she is seriously questioning if the dream of the corner office is really that lofty a goal.

Yesterday, she decided to take her 3-year-old son and 4-month-old baby girl on an outing. She had 1 week until her maternity leave came to an end, the skies were blue in Portland (a rarity), and she itched for the chance to bond with both kids before she officially returned to her stressful position. Her son had been requesting a trip to the gondola that connects Oregon Health and Science University's waterfront and mountain campuses for weeks so he could see the special engine room. "Today," she decided, "is the day," preparing herself with all the gear necessary for potential diaper blowouts, toddler snack requests, and weather changes.

On her arrival to the gondola engine room, baby June immediately started fussing. "No problem," she thought, reaching for a pacifier from her bag. But June was not interested in the pacifier or in multiple attempts at nursing in a crowded room. Katie fumbled with the nursing cover and her wriggly baby, who grew more and more unsatisfied in her arms by the minute. She shushed, she swayed, she swaddled, but June was having none of it. After 10 minutes of full-tilt screaming, Katie decided it was time to call it quits.

"Sorry, buddy," she explained to her son Carter. "Sister doesn't feel good. We have to come back another day to see the gondola. Can you be a patient big brother and be nice to June on the way home? She will probably still cry a little as we drive."

He looked up at his mama with sad eyes but nodded and started walking toward the car.

June cried at the top of her lungs the entire 26-minute ride back across town. Carter sat silent in the back. Katie was never so happy to see her driveway, but the day's challenges were not over. As she tried to handle all of her gear and a still-screaming baby while getting out of the car, she asked Carter to bring his sippy cup into the house.

"No, mommy, you bring it," he responded.

She took a deep breath and tried to be logical. "OK, Carter. If you don't want to bring your cup in, you have to leave it in the car. Mommy can't carry it right now. Her hands are full, and June is really unhappy."

"No, *you* bring it!" he yelled.

"I can't, Carter. I am sorry."

That was not the response he was hoping for. He dropped his toy onto the ground, glared at his mom and opened his mouth.

"Aggghhhhhh!" Now he, too, was screaming at the top of his lungs and would not stop.

In that moment Katie wanted to scream louder than the 2 of her children combined. A family walking down the street with their dog looked on judgingly as they passed her yard.

Already exhausted, Katie dropped her bags and carried one fussy baby into the house in her car safety seat and one screaming toddler in by the waist.

"You left my water in the car, Mommy!" Carter sobbed until she calmed him. "You...left...my...water." Which really meant, *I am so disappointed that we had to leave the gondola and that my sister ruined it for all of us and that you wouldn't even do the one thing I asked you to do*, but how can you ask a toddler to explain all that? Even he didn't realize the real cause for his tantrum.

With one child now playing quietly with his toys, Katie worked on calming her daughter, which took a few hours and a call to her daughter's pediatrician to finally accomplish. Did she have an ear infection? Was she just overtired? Only several days later, when 2 tiny teeth emerged on her daughter's gums, did she get the satisfaction of hindsight.

Katie called it one of her worst parenting experiences, and it would have been bad enough if that was her only struggle of the day. It turns out, though, that her peer and personal friend from work had called earlier that morning. She mentioned some bad news about a project Katie had spent the better part of 2 years working on as they caught up about all things new baby and motherhood. The project was set to launch a month after she returned from leave. Her colleague had taken over in her absence and, quite frankly, had dropped the ball. She was, it seemed, in a hot panic to let Katie know how bad things were on the team.

As she took the call, Katie realized that her options were either to end her maternity leave early by diving back into work mode immediately or to preserve her last moments of family time, challenging her colleague to step up, even if the project results were not nearly what she hoped they would be. She was conflicted. This project was her brainchild. She would be held accountable for its finished product. She had poured her heart and soul into it, but she was also trying to pour her heart and soul into her kids. Judging from the day's events, her oldest would need even more TLC than she originally thought when she transitioned back to work.

Katie, like me, is constantly evaluating and recalibrating where to place her efforts and her time, depending on her own individual needs and the needs of her family. She felt conflicted in that moment—a moment when she had to choose between going back to work and staying home—and she feels conflicted a lot of the time. She's conflicted about what she wants for herself and for her children, but she's also conflicted about how she fits into a world that demands that she *lean in* if she wants to participate at all professionally. She hears the messaging loud and clear: *especially before you become a mother, lean in as far as you can until the very last second. Then make sure to not lean out once the baby arrives.*

Modern working moms strive every day in the workplace. They're just as ambitious as they've always been about the things they care most about, but I hear a powerful cry from the working mothers who surround me. They want more. They're looking for a way to navigate the working mom world with a little more ease and joy (and a lot less frustration), but they're confused about how to do it.

I understand their conundrum because I've been there myself.

✂✂✂✂

I was born committed. When I'm in on something, I'm *all* in. At the age of 9, I marched into my living room and announced boldly that I'd finalized my plans to open a business. We lived across the valley from a horse stable and I decided one day, watching a mare with her foal in the distance from my window, that grooming and feeding ponies on Saturdays would be the perfect way to fund my Barbie collection. My brother, who was lining up GI Joes for fake battle on the floor, looked up at me and rolled his eyes. My dad, who was reclined in his easy chair, watching football and reading the paper at the same time, put the local news section down and smiled. "If anyone can do it, you can, sweetie," he said encouragingly.

I hand-drew paper advertisements for my services and delivered them neighbor by neighbor the next day. "If Saturdays don't work for you, just let me know," I told the woman next door eagerly. "I could come by after school with carrots or could even stop in after church on Sundays." I begged my dad to drive me to the stable owner's office so I could pitch my business there too. "I'm a hard worker. I'm even willing to muck the stalls," I told him when he promised to spread the word to his customers.

In junior high school, my friend Lisa and I decided to enter a contest for *Seventeen Magazine*. The publication was looking for contributions about friendship—an essay, a creative project—anything that highlighted what being a good friend was all about. The prize was a lifetime subscription to *Seventeen* and $100 for each participant. Lisa and I had known each other since birth. We had a lot to say on the subject but, instead of writing about our history together, we decided to make an artistic, visual representation of our bond. We designed a real-life cardboard gift box with fold-down sides and a ribbon bow that held it all together. Each side had 3D photos and drawings picturing our years together in ballet classes, at summer camps, and playing with our siblings in our backyards. Lisa and I painstakingly wrapped it up and shipped it off for review. We didn't win, but we must have taken a thousand pictures of our creation, we were so proud of our dedication to our work.

At 16, after watching a spinal fusion surgery on a career day field trip, I decided I wanted to be a doctor. The kind of doctor I wanted to be, though, was the kind that wrote in magazine columns and explained medicine on television (in addition to seeing patients). A journalism degree, I learned as I poured over career guides at Barnes and Noble and via dial-up internet at home, was one way to the evening news. Instead of majoring in biology or chemistry, I would take a less traditional route to medical school. To complete all of the prerequisite courses I needed and still graduate in 4 years, I had to do some advance planning. I still remember the poster board grid I created to map out my college career. I affixed tiny Velcro course labels to it and shuffled them around the board each semester depending on my ability to register for the classes I needed. There was no question in my mind that, if I worked hard enough at it, I could make it happen.

I continued that commitment to diligence and focused energy as a practicing physician. I leaned in to the working world. Someone needed to stay a little late to see a toddler with a high fever on a Tuesday night? My partners could count on me. The group needed someone to lead a com-mittee? I was their girl. An urgent email came through and needed to be answered immediately? No problem. I was happy to do what it took to be a team player and to advance my own career. I caught up on relaxation and rejuvenation on the weekends, hanging out with friends and sleeping in whenever I wanted to.

I went full-force professionally because I wanted to prove myself a worthy employee and because I wanted to succeed. I love my work and I wanted a seat at the table, as Sheryl Sandberg put it in her groundbreaking book, *Lean In*. I knew there were generations of women who paved the way in the working world before me with single-minded grit so I *had* the opportunity to even be a doctor in the first place. I respected that and wanted that for myself too.

Then I had a baby girl and everything changed when it came to being "all in." My daughter suffered from severe colic. She struggled with potty training. She had the hardest time sleeping. She tantrumed all the way through her tod-dler years. She lashed out whenever she was emotionally dysregulated. She suffered from the very first month of her life under what I know now was an extreme level of anxiety.

My daughter has grown into a creative force who feels deeply and cares immensely; a brilliant mind who loves reading, imagining, and expressing. In her best moments, she is a light to everyone — happily singing and dancing. She cuddles in close for hugs and stories. She joyfully leads her sister in plays and dress-up performances. But those moments were often hard to come by in her early years and could be shrouded by worry and fight-or-flight–fueled reactions in the blink of an eye.

As a pediatrician, I know all kids sometimes have trouble regulating their emotions, especially when they're tired or hungry or scared, but this was something completely different. There were so many nights all I could do was sit against the door inside her bedroom as she raged over an unpredicted turn of events ("No, mommy I can't go if Matt won't be there! I don't care if he's sick.") or over worries that wouldn't let her be ("What if I make a mistake in dance class? I just can't go! Everyone will laugh at me."). We worked with her pediatrician, with psychologists, with occupational therapists, with parent coaches — even eventually with a psychiatrist— to support her. Sometimes, it felt like her needs defined her, no, *consumed* her — and me.

My daughter and my family needed their mom's full commitment, but my professional obligations at work continued to pull at me as well. In fact, the more senior I became in my job, the more pressure I felt to be "all in," even when I really couldn't be. We had another daughter and, as the 2 girls grew older, life got even more complicated. There were school supplies to buy, music classes to sign up for, playdates to join, laundry to fold, doctors' appointments to schedule — times 2. Things got chaotic real fast being a working mother of 2.

I felt the push and pull of my life acutely. I was conflicted and guilty no matter where I placed my efforts. I was like a yo-yo on a string, swinging from one direction to another, a study in extremes. I felt guilty that my kids took away from my work responsibilities, so I pushed harder professionally. When I leaned into work, I found myself feeling like a bad mom, and I was tempted to overindulge my children when I got home. I felt guilty about the fact I wasn't home with them every day. Even when it came to caring for myself, I did so reactively. "I need a break!" I'd say to my husband on Saturday afternoons and spend hours after the kids were in bed bingeing on cable television series or scrolling all night through Instagram.

Sure, I *could* do it all. I was a jedi at juggling everything: work, home, my social obligations. You name it, I could fit it in, make it happen, or mop it up. But I started to question *if* doing it all was worth it because, I realized, in trying to do it all one big thing was missing: joy and contentment. I hardly ever felt centered and aligned. I was constantly conflicted—pulled every which way, all at the same time. I forced my career and my mothering to fit together in my life by doing *more* constantly—staying up late most nights to answer emails I couldn't get to during the day, spending time on car rides in the passengers seat with my family ordering toothpaste and toilet paper for our home, fitting in responses to lingering personal texts on the way to or from a meeting or an after-school activity. I was strong—fierce, even, in the eyes of the world—but I didn't feel very solid inside myself. I *had* to make a change. I too was burned out to do anything else. Like so many other working moms around me, even those without such an extreme situation with their child, I started yearning for a better version of my motherhood experience.

Mary Beth Ferrante, CEO of Live.Work.Lead. and ardent supporter of millennial working women, wrote the following in a 2018 *Forbes* magazine article:

Millennial mothers are feeling overwhelmed and unsupported during the transition from motherhood to working mother. Our disenchantment with integrating motherhood and work undermines the expectations of our generation. No previous generation has applied more effort in creating a harmonious co-existence between work and life. For Baby Boomers and Gen X, it was normal to draw a line in the sand and expect family life and work to be separate. But with technology significantly changing the way we work today and into the future, it is increasingly difficult to separate the two. Our ability, and now expectation, to respond to emails late into the evenings and weekends, has us wondering why flexible hours are still something to negotiate, or why we feel judged when we leave the office at 5pm to pick up our children, even though we are often getting to work hours earlier than others.

I decided I had to break the cycle of burnout I was experiencing if I ever wanted to experience more centeredness for myself, and that meant changes at home and at work. I had to figure out a way to navigate the working mom world with more intentionality, to move from overindulgence or small, stolen moments as my only form of self-care to a pledge to make space for myself and my needs in a sustainable, consistent way. From a lean in mentality at work to a decision to say yes when it made sense for me and my family and to say no when it really didn't. From acting resentful and haughty when my partner didn't share my mental or household duty load to actually working toward more equity between us. From operating out of guilt when my kids begged for me to spend all day, every day with them to showing up for them regularly with attunement and connection. I wanted a life that was richer and more fulfilling, that didn't drain me at every turn and in both roles.

CONFESSIONS FROM WORKING MOMS: My friend Katie feels the same way. She believes in "taking a seat at the table" when she's there, but she's not sure she wants to be at the table all the time. She believes in pushing aggressively for equal treatment and equal opportunities for women and for men, but she wants her partnership with her spouse to also be harmonious, not a battlefield or a tally sheet. She wants to be a great mother, but she cares about her professional dreams too. She doesn't believe that women should have to lean in so far in any one direction or in so many directions that they push themselves beyond their limits and sacrifice their own emotional well-being or the emotional well-being of the people they love best. She believes that alignment and centeredness matter most. She's done with single-minded grit—and so am I.

Chapter 2

Working Moms Today
A Study in Trade-offs and Benefits

*Just trying to figure out how to balance being a mother of
a six-year-old and twins that need me, and giving myself
creatively and physically, there's a lot to juggle.*

—Beyoncé

A few years ago, a woman brought her daughter
into my pediatrics office for her 15-year well-
child visit.

"What do you want to be when you grow up?" I asked.

She smiled at me and looked at her mom nervously. "A
lawyer. A high-profile criminal prosecutor."

Her mom beamed. Her sense of pride for her daughter
was like a waterfall held back by a thin edge of stones, ready
to burst out. You could tell this was the ultimate level of
achievement for their family. I asked the young girl why she
chose law and why she was particularly interested in that area
of specialization within the legal field. She straightened up,
rolled her shoulders back, and brightened her eyes, leaning
forward toward me.

"I'm a really good student, and I know lawyers are really
important. It's the top of the top. Really, nothing else matters
to me," she said.

I felt myself react almost physically. Those were probably
the exact words I used when people queried me in high
school about my plans to pursue medicine. The words jarred

me back 20 years, but her delivery of them was even more recognizable. I saw my sincere eagerness in her intent eyes. Like, *I will do this. I will rise to the top no matter what. Dare to stop me. Nothing else matters.* Of course, at that time, I didn't have the foresight to understand or consider how family life complicates a career path, nor should I have. There's no way I could have known that, as a mother, a lot of other things would matter—namely, the 2 beautiful daughters I brought into the world. It was impossible to see then that, if I wanted happiness *and* success as a working mom, I would have to deal with the demands that come with both those jobs. Most importantly, I couldn't see that joy, connection, and contentment mattered above all else.

When I was young, my mom worked hard to carefully balance her role as a mother and as an independent businesswoman. She worked as a solo entrepreneur, running her own start-up gift sales company until I was 11, and then went to work as an art gallery director for a busy, commercial firm. Often, she balanced work and motherhood well, but sometimes it was hard to manage. Sometimes, doing 1 job well meant sacrificing the other.

I vividly remember my brother and I were arguing one morning while my mom placed a business call. She tried to silently shush us 3 times as we chased and yelled at each other back and forth in the hallway. Finally, exasperated and red-faced, she spoke into the phone sweetly, trying to keep herself together.

"Hold please," she said, muting the other end of the line and turning toward us.

"If you 2 do not settle down and behave yourselves, there will be time-outs. And, if you cannot behave in time-out, just wait until your father comes home!"

She reached out to slam the door and glared (or was it really pleading, I wonder years later), returning to her phone conversation.

"Hmmm, um, excuse me. Where were we?...Oh, yes, so that is what we call our executive package...."

It did not happen often. My mom was a saint, trying to take care of us all day, worrying about balance sheets and gift shows at the same time. My dad was supportive and progressive, taking on a significant amount of the child care responsibilities while he worked full time teaching high school, but she still did the majority of the housework and child care, trying to balance her professional life with her family life. Her ability to reach her business goals was, whether she liked it or not, always affected by her goal to mother well. When those 2 worlds were at odds, you could see the stress on my mother's face. She had to learn, like every working mom does at some point, if she wants to move from a state of persistent inner conflict to a state of consistent centeredness, how to balance her efforts between work and home. First she needs to recognize her guilt, using it as a chance to analyze what she needed and we needed most at each decision point, and then making priority-based decisions to place more emphasis in one area or the other depending on the given situation. Sometimes that meant staying up late at night working on client invoices so she could spend more focused time with us during the day. Sometimes that meant missing a baseball game or two for my brother so she could attend a really important meeting. Sometimes it meant cancelling her whole morning of appointments so we could go out to breakfast, just the 2 of us.

I feel the same way she did during that business phone call as I field my own calls at home for my pediatric practice every few weeks. A few days ago, I was literally trying to balance my 2 worlds as I talked to a mom on the phone about a chicken noodle soup burn to her child's leg while holding my own restless child on my lap. My husband had his own work meeting that night, leaving me solo with the kids. The littlest one was unaware she was screaming into the phone as she clawed at my face with her small hands to get my attention, unsettled and clearly feeling ignored during what was usually mommy time.

"Hold on just a sec, I just have to get my baby happy and distracted for a minute so I can concentrate," I explained to the anxious mom.

"Sure," she said. "Sorry to take time away from your family tonight."

I felt guilty, overwhelmed, and flustered—all at the same time. The mom on the phone likely appreciated I could empathize with her fears about her daughter's leg but sensed the pediatrician in me couldn't give her my full attention. My own child obviously wanted more of me too. I knew I was doing the best I could in that moment, but I also knew it wasn't enough for anyone, including myself.

Modern working moms like me are so often caught in the middle. They have a multitude of responsibilities and expectations, both at work and at home, and the mental overload that comes with keeping all those balls in the air is exhausting. Most mamas I know have a sneaking suspicion that, even though they're supposed to be it all and do it all, they're not really doing *any* of it that well in the end.

EJ Dickson, millennial mother, writer, and editor, summed it up in her *Bustle* article: "I am constantly frustrated and frazzled, and—to be honest—angry that having children and a career is still such a heroic feat."

Working women want to have more equal co-parenting partnerships but, in most households, they still carry the mental load of home care and family care, even though they may live with a partner and both partners may be working full time. At work, they're trying to lean in, but they are hindered by their personal responsibilities outside the office or by institutional bias. They miss their children and feel like they're missing out on opportunities to connect with their kids and their kids' worlds throughout the week. And, as the try to care for themselves in the midst of all the other factors to consider, they're hit with an extreme amount of guilt.

The more I talk with other working moms about their struggles to find balance, though, the more I sense something even deeper than guilt happening to this generation of mothers. There, underneath their day-to-day stress and fatigue, is genuine disappointment with how motherhood and life are going.

I understand their predicament well. My husband and I ordered a special celebratory dinner the night my first book, *The New Baby Blueprint*, was published. It was an important professional milestone for me, and I was proud of all the hard work it took to get to that moment.

"Come on, guys," he called up to my girls from the kitchen when the boxes of curry and spring rolls arrived. "Your mom just got home from the office and it's time to eat. Let's party. Your mom has a book out!"

My little one came bounding down the stairs, wearing some kind of cowgirl-meets-international princess ensemble. She climbed up on her chair and started digging into the rice on the plate in front of her.

"Good job, mommy," she said through full bites of food. "Is there cake?"

My 6-year-old sauntered down our first flight of stairs and into the dining room, looking less than enthusiastic about her dinner options but very interested in the latest family news.

"Does that mean since you have the book out now you're done with working, like for forever? Will tomorrow be a mommy-daughter day and all the days after that? Can you stop being a doctor now?"

It would have been easy to cave inward from the weight of that question. She was genuine in her ask and my reaction was sincere too. When she asked me to never leave her side, it fed into an ingrained belief I see so many women struggle with. It's a belief that to be a good mom I need to be completely devoted to my children—above my work, above myself—above every other area of my life.

The next day at my pediatrics office, the opposite scenario ensued. At our monthly medical professional meeting one of my partners passed around a sign-up sheet with a list of committee and volunteer opportunities.

"I want to remind everyone that this is not a lifestyle practice," one of my partners voiced to the room. "Our work goes beyond clocking in at 9:00 am and clocking out at 5:00 pm. We each have to pull our weight. We need every person to pick up the slack and, right now, we really need more committee members—as many as possible."

With the book newly published and my daughter's comments fresh in my mind from the night before, I hesitated to add my name to the list but knew it might draw criticism from my business partners. I felt the same pressure all the other moms I know feel to be a good worker—someone who's fully committed to my colleagues and my corporation, the kind of person who takes care of my personal life on my personal time, who doesn't let family considerations interfere with my professional pursuits or efforts. The problem is, those 2 ideals, the good mother and the professional worker, both fully committed and laser focused on their tasks, are at odds with one another, creating not just guilt but stress too. It's the pursuit of both ideals at the same time, of perfection as we mother *and* as we strive professionally, that's making it all feel like so much of a letdown. We're having a horrible time because, somewhere along the line, we get bogged down in fake ideals of seeking the perfect balance. If we can move beyond those unattainable fantasies, though, and see working motherhood as the ultimate example of accepting trade-offs and benefits, we find ourselves in a unique position that, in the end, offers huge benefits to our kids.

I decided, in the end, to join 1 work committee — the one with the lowest time commitment and the least amount of energy required. When my kids are older and I'm in a different life stage, I'll commit to more (maybe) and, if I do, it won't be to fit a good worker ideal. It will be based on what my company needs *and* what works well for me at the time.

"Well," I told my daughter that next night at the table. "Something interesting happened today. Mommy had to be strong so I could do what was best for you and for me. Here's the thing, sweetie. I can't stop working…but I also don't want to stop working. I love you and your sister so much, and, at the same time, I love helping people. I want to use the special way I'm wired to help people who don't live here with us too. What I *can* do is make sure we have plenty of opportunities to be together doing all the things we love and being connected with each other."

"OK," she said, taking it all in. Then, she brightened. "Actually, can I help? I know! I can make signs around the neighborhood telling new moms we can help them feel less scared about having their babies."

My pride in her resilience puffed up like a balloon. *See? I thought. Like me, she struggled initially with accepting that her vision of me connected at the hip all day, every day is unrealistic, but she was able to problem solve through it. By choosing a more middle road, I'm teaching her she can do the same when she's older and in my shoes.*

As working women, we have an opportunity to be an example of living with passion and priorities, of working hard, of staying committed, not necessarily to work itself but to the priorities we set around our work and our personal lives. When we work and parent simultaneously, we have a chance to teach our kids resilience — letting our kids see that even if they struggle with something they can handle it and get stronger from it — and to embrace a village mentality, not in a better way than stay-at-home moms can but in a very different way.

Above all, we have the unique pleasure of encouraging our own kids to find real balance and real joy as they live their lives and as they go on to work and parent the next generation. By the way, that's what I wanted to say to that law school–bound teenager in my office—that it's all about joy, so aim for that over accomplishment—but it came out something like, "You do you, and maybe that's going to be law, but choose joy first and foremost." I'm sure her mom was confused. I've got to work on my speech for the next time it comes up.

It comes down to this: working moms like you and me don't need a 10-step, how-to organizational plan for cramming it all into a day, only to end up exhausted and furious. Working moms need a realistic guide to balancing their work and their lives, focused on taking care of the social-emotional needs of their kids and themselves. If we want to be successful, we have to get real about what really matters, setting realistic expectations and practicing self-compassion, while proactively managing guilt and anxiety. In the next chapter, we'll start learning how.

Chapter 3

You Can't Have It All

Things which matter most must never be at the mercy of things which matter least.

—Johann Wolfgang von Goethe

WHAT THE WORLD SAYS I NEED TO DO TO BE A GOOD WORKING MOM:
Lean in at work. Lean in so hard you think you can't lean in any further. Then lean in some more. Make sure your colleagues can count on you. It's not enough to be a part of the team—make sure you have a front seat at the proverbial work table. Fight for equal pay by showing them you deserve it. Don't let them see your weaknesses or your insecurities. You've got to "man up." Take the lead. Speak up in meetings and take charge in your decision-making. Take every opportunity they give you. If you feel like you're about to break, you're doing it right.

This is especially important when you have a newborn. If you choose to breastfeed, you're going to need to pump at work. Every day. Every 3 hours. If that seems like a lot, don't worry, there are laws to protect this special time—I'm sure your employer will follow them to a T without any pushback. The time may not feel special because, instead of having a tiny infant suckling at your nipples, 2 giant cones attached to a suction machine will be milking you like a cow at a corporate dairy farm. Enjoy your free time while you're pumping, though. Or, better yet, get some work done—you don't want to fall behind your male partners.

When it comes to free time, it's so important to take full advantage of it. Every spare moment you have is a chance to get something else done, to make a check mark on your to-do list. If you're organized and focused enough, this shouldn't be an issue. Make sure you keep up to date on all the new apps designed specifically to make balancing your work and home life as efficient as possible. You might need to get up an hour earlier than everyone else in your family every day, including weekends, to make your hard work pay off.

Speaking of sleep, you really need it. Don't skimp. Take care of yourself by getting to bed at a reasonable hour each night. Never mind the laundry piling up, the dishes in the sink, or the 30-minute Netflix comedy special you've been waiting all day to enjoy. They can wait. Sleep matters most. Unless your kid wakes up and needs you. You don't want them to develop a separation anxiety issue. After all, you are a working mom—you need to spend as much time with your child as possible—even if it means you show up to work a little haggard.

Appearance. Super important. Sorry, you may be modern, but the world will still judge you on one thing first as a woman: your looks. So, make sure you look polished at all times and you wear Spanx if you haven't gotten back to your pre-baby body by 3 months postpartum. Though you really should be able to fit in all your prepregnancy outfits by then. If not people *will* talk. Even your friends.

Oh yeah, friends. You're going to need them. Never mind that you've forgotten how to hold a conversation about anything other than baby spit-up. This is *the time* to connect with other moms and, if you don't do it in the next few years, everyone will already be all buddy-buddy with each other and you'll miss out. In fact, it could seriously affect your child's networking opportunities as they look into employ-ment options down the road.

By the way, you'd better start looking into ways to prep your toddler for college admission now. These days, it's very competitive. You're going to want to sign your child up for piano (or violin) lessons as soon as they become available—the younger the better! Sports are an absolute must too. Maybe your kid will get a scholarship if he's better than everyone else on the team. How else are you going to pay for his education? Don't push too hard on the athletics, though. Your child could grow up to resent you and hate you if you overstress him or if you don't challenge him enough. There's only a small margin for error either way.

If you can, volunteer whenever possible. Who cares that you're working?! You have a whole hour at lunch available—that's the perfect time to drive across town to participate in this month's Halloween, Valentine's, May Day, or Just Because It's Tuesday celebration at the elementary school. This is *your child* we're talking about, after all. You can never get this once-in-a-lifetime memory back again.

Memories! Pay special attention to making every Christmas morning and Easter basket as memorable as possible. After all, Susie's mom down the street is at home every day making milk and cookies. You (please remember or I will need to remind you again) are not. This is the least you can do for your poor kid—she's missing out on so many other bonding moments with you. Search Pinterest for hours until you find the best handmade rainbow unicorn birthday cake recipe to serve at your sweet angel's celebration—the one that requires buying a special pan for $59 even though you have 80 pans in your pantry. This should be easy for you. You are a woman, right? Baking should come naturally to you, as should folding underwear and interior decorating.

Which reminds me, you need to keep a spotless house. Make sure it's perfectly organized and clean. What if someone comes over? Of course, it may take 5 hours to scrub from top to bottom, but what else could you possibly be spending your time on that you can't make more of an effort in this area?

Don't forget to spend time on yourself, though. You don't want a major illness, do you? Better make it every year to the doctor for a Pap smear and a skin check. Also, work in exercise 7 days a week, make your own farm-fresh, 5-course meals, drink 8 glasses of water a day, and go to therapy. Go even if it's not covered by insurance. Some things must be put to the top of your list! Don't go into debt over it, though. That will really mess you up.

Oh, couples care! This is critical. Get a babysitter! But go out after your kids go to sleep so you don't steal time away from them to make it happen. They need you! You've been gone all day and they miss you, remember? So what if you're too tired at 9:00 pm to hit the town? Your marriage depends on this! Sometimes you have to push yourself to your limits to make time for what matters. Stay sexy. Resentment is unattractive. Who cares if you're doing way more than half of the work to make your family's life run? That's just the way it is. There are even studies to prove it. You can do anything for 18 short years. Suck it up.

Above all else, stay balanced and happy and content. After all, this is the life you always dreamed of. You're just going to need to work a little harder to make it a reality.

෨෬෨෬

WHAT I SAY BACK: If having it all means missing out on what matters, I'm out. If leaning in means sacrificing joy and contentment, I quit. If working so hard to achieve perfect balance means I never make it to my top priorities, I just can't abide. I'm tired of performing.

Modern Mommy Doc
December 16, 2019 · 🌐

Mama, I'm not willing to lose myself, my authentic relationships with my children, my love for my partner or my sanity for some version of happiness someone else defines...and neither should you. It's time to learn how to truly win at parenting without losing ourselves.

XO,

Dr. Whitney

Modern Mommy Doc. Facebook. Posted December 16, 2019. https://www.facebook.com/modernmommydoc/photos/how-to-be-a-good-working-mom-according-to-the-worldthe-world-keeps-telling-meyou/637375873466407

Why did this Facebook post for my Modern Mommy Doc community resonate with so many other working women trying to raise babies and young kids out there? Because even as society bombards us with tips and tricks for doing it all, we sense deep down it's an impossible feat. Something about the responses from the moms who read it gives me hope that I'm not alone in this feeling of impossibility when it comes to doing modern "mommyhood" well. Something about it also gets me thinking. Did we make the wrong choice when we chose to pursue careers and motherhood simultaneously? Can you be successful or happy as a working mom and find balance? *Yes.* Just not all the time in every way.

I know the media tells you otherwise. I know it seems like you *should* be having it all. But look at your life. Do you have it all now? Even when you've tried your best at it? Even without kids? I didn't. I could never look exactly the way I wanted *and* be the best at my job *and* always have a hopping social calendar *and* travel the world *and* have tons of money in the bank *and* be peaceful and happy all the time at the same time. Anyone who tries to sell you otherwise is selling you lies (*The New Baby Blueprint: Caring for You and Your Little One.* 2020:42).

Remember, that's the world's lie to everyone, but especially to working moms. Every decision we make includes a trade-off and a benefit.

჋ჿ჋ჿ჋ჿ

CONFESSIONS FROM WORKING MOMS: My friend Christie is a business executive coach. She spends all day guiding leaders personally and professionally as they make million-dollar decisions. One night, while we were out discussing life, she took a napkin and wrote out the major categories of life— kids, partner, work, exercise, friendships, hobbies, homemaking, travel and experiences, and appearance. For clarification, exercise to me meant releasing endorphins, stress reduction, and meditation, whereas appearance included everything that goes into looking put together (including exercise for the purpose of having a good appearance).

She wrote them in random order and then asked me to rank them in order in the left-hand column according to what I, in an ideal world, would spend the most time doing. "Rank them as a private, honest list, not based at all on what other people would think is the right way to rank them," she said.

I called it my Ideal List.

IDEAL LIST
1. Exercise and stress reduction
2. Kids
3. Travel and experiences
4. Hobbies and sports (including writing and reading)
5. Partner
6. Friendships
7. Homemaking (tasks such as laundry and dishes)
8. Appearance
9. Work

In the next column, she asked me to rank what I thought I spent my time on.

Here is my Reality List.

REALITY LIST
1. Work
2. Homemaking
3. Kids
4. Hobbies and sports
5. Partner
6. Appearance
7. Friendships
8. Exercise and stress reduction
9. Travel and experiences

Then, she told me to compare them.

| My Comparison List of Major Life Categories—Side by Side ||
Ideal	Reality
1. Exercise and stress reduction	1. Work
2. Kids	2. Homemaking
3. Travel and experiences	3. Kids
4. Hobbies and sports	4. Hobbies and sports
5. Partner	5. Partner
6. Friendships	6. Appearance
7. Homemaking	7. Friendships
8. Appearance	8. Exercise and stress reduction
9. Work	9. Travel and experiences

Look at the striking comparison between what my ideal
life looked like and what my actual life looked like. This
exercise is what convinced me to make a change in my life.
Also, notice that although my kids ranked high on the list,

they were not first. That's OK. In fact, it's probably healthier. Because, in the end, my kids are going to grow up and do their own thing (yours will too). My husband was also not first. That's OK too. It's important we have separate interests and desires, which we can build only if we spend some time doing things separately.

You might be thinking, "I'm going to have to work!" That's true for me too. That's how I pay for all the music classes, the nanny, and the nutritious quality food I want to provide for my kids in the first place. It's how my daughter goes to that fun preschool. It's how we make sure we get to live in the house we do and get our kids into the great schools that they go to. There is not going to be some overhaul of my life that allows me to live work free and spend all day sipping lattes while I supervise my children.

Also, you might have a different top 3 on your Ideal List than I do, and that is totally fine. This exercise is for you. My husband is a huge extrovert. I had him make this list, and his was in a completely different order than mine. No problem. That's the beauty of it.

I'm not saying don't go to work or don't figure out a way to get your house clean, but, as my friend says, "Work is like a parasite. It will leach out of you as much as you will give to it." So is creating a life filled with a whole lot of ways to keep yourself busy and distracted but with hardly any meaningful experiences.

Of course, work can also be intellectually and personally fulfilling—a way to exercise all of our talents—and, even if housecleaning, grocery shopping, and coordinating 80 million schedules are less fulfilling to us than our professional careers, we still have to do some of these things to keep our lives running smoothly. The point is not to throw them to the wayside altogether; it's to figure out a way to keep them from sucking the life out of us. The rest of the things on the list you'll have to consider like gravy or a cherry on top if

you can get to them, at least in the early years of motherhood. It's OK if your makeup isn't perfect, your socks aren't
organized, and you can't remember the last time you cooked
something more complicated than a quesadilla.

It's especially important for working moms to pick their
top 3 priorities and focus on them because we have *fewer
free hours in the day to focus on them than other moms do*. We
have more to juggle in the first place. If we want to do any
of it well, we have to pick and choose.

Truly Living According to Our Priorities

I know firsthand about living according to your priorities
because I haven't always been able to. For the first 15 years
of my marriage, my husband and I carried around a heavy
burden. We felt stuck and trapped, limited in our options
and choices. We made decisions based on what we had to
do versus what worked well for us as a family.

My husband Scott and I were college sweethearts. We
met in animal biology class and fell in love over scalpels
and forceps in dissection anatomy lab, talking for endless
hours about our families and our futures. We got married
after we graduated—still young and naive to the pitfalls of
money troubles and chronic stress. Three weeks after we
said, "I do," armed with a truck full of wedding presents and
2 credit cards, we started driving across the country to start
our respective graduate programs in medicine and physical
therapy at the University of Vermont.

Although my doctoring dream was planned and anticipated, my husband's opportunity to pursue a career in health
care came fast and furious. He'd always been interested in
physical therapy but didn't have his heart set on it. Almost
magically, it seemed at the time, the university's physical therapy department offered Scott a last-minute spot in
their 3-year program when we visited 4 months before my
start date to check out rental properties. It felt like all signs

pointed to saying yes, never mind the financial implications of starting our marriage as 2 full-time graduate students with no income outside of financial aid.

We paid close attention to money from the very beginning. I can still remember living frugally in graduate school—we moved into cramped subsidized student housing and ate Costco samples for lunch almost every Sunday as we struggled to live off the loans we took out simultaneously to cover tuition, housing, and living expenses. We lived month to month. We were both considered out of state during our entire graduate school tenure and, at the end, racked up *way* over 6 figures to make our educational pursuits happen.

I remember the student loan officers droning on about compounding interest when we signed the loan paperwork. I remember thinking we were living as minimally as possible (well, maybe not as minimally as possible—we went out on date nights with our friends and took a few trips with my family—but not extravagantly, by any means). Above all else, I remember thinking that I was working this hard because I was becoming a doctor and that doctors make good money and that, in the end, we would be just fine. I understood I would be tied for at least 15 years to my career choice, but I thought that, someday, I would pay it all off.

Fast-forward more than a decade: I was a seasoned practitioner at my clinic, a mom of 2, and a homeowner. My husband was the director of his physical therapy clinic. I was right in the sweet spot of my career, and I'd made it through the trenches of infancy with both of my girls. When I thought about moving forward with a speaking and writing career, though, to finding a better sense of balance, I was still hamstrung by the financial implications of the choices we made (frankly, as children) in our early marriage experience.

We'd paid off some of the debt. Slowly, our student loan bills were starting to decrease, but the rest of our expenses were rising as we added more people (and their stuff) to our already full lives. Child care cost us a pretty penny. A mortgage in a metropolitan city was not cheap. Something had to give.

Given the rainy weather in Portland, we always plan a spring trip to clear out the seasonal blues and to get some sunshine as a family. We made our way to the beach that March—to a simple place with a porch looking out over the ocean.

I was sitting on a deck chair one morning with my child, drinking a cup of coffee and feeling wistful about my life, when I had the kind of epiphany that comes only once in a great while—maybe only once or twice in a lifetime. My sweet girl was wrapped up tight on my lap, her little legs folded against my belly, her eyes closed, her head resting on my chest. I realized, sitting there looking out over the blue water that stretched out forever in front of me, that, even with someone else pressed as tightly as possible to me, the word that best defined that moment was *freedom*. I craved the freedom to have simple moments of serenity with my kids and with myself. I wanted to be able to choose, not every second or even every day, but definitely over the course of my existence, how I lived my life and spent my time. I wanted freedom to truly live according to my priorities, in a way that felt centered, not so conflicted all the time.

After that beach trip, we made a major life change. We'd always tried to shop smart and save money, but, this time, we made some radical decisions in an effort to open up our life options. We moved into my parents' house for 12 months and rented out our own home, saving thousands of dollars a month by mitigating our mortgage costs and lowering our utility bills. We changed our child care situation, dropping nanny hours and changing our own work schedules around to accommodate school drop-offs and pickups. We committed to staycations and clearance rack–only shopping trips for a year while we got aggressive about reducing our debt. We put every bonus dollar we received toward loan repayment. In the end, we paid down over a third of our debt and set ourselves up to continue working toward financial freedom.

I understand that when my husband and I decided to make a major life change, we had a secure safety net below us. I realize we were lucky enough to have our house in the first place. Without having our house which we decided to rent, we wouldn't have been able to save that much money in such a short period of time. And as equally as important we had my parents and a whole circle of friends and family who supported us.

All those factors made our experience safer, but it didn't make our experience any less difficult. My husband had to live with his in-laws for a full year (he loves them, but it was not his first choice). We had nowhere to hide when our kids acted out or when we had our own marital squabbles. Because we were saving money, I quit spending my dollars on any frivolous comforts I would have previously turned to on a hard day or week. Life got real *really* quick.

Why am I sharing this with you? Maybe you have no debt. Maybe you don't feel stuck financially but you do feel stuck in the type of work you're doing, or you feel stuck in your child care situation, or in the hubbub of your life as a mom and a worker and a partner.

What I decided to do to get free goes beyond my individual story. It goes beyond my specific financial situation. When I talked to friends and acquaintances about my family's plan, almost every single person who heard about it responded by either telling me feverishly about some major adjustment they'd also made at some point in their lives for the better or explained wistfully why they'd like to make a similar change in an unhealthy personal relationship, a stress-inducing work environment, or their own financial fitness but just couldn't because of x, y, or z.

Living according to your own priorities applies to every single working mother out there. When I see the shares and comments on my post about society's motherhood ideals, it tells me that we all feel stuck, in some way or another, and that the only real way out is to make some hard (or at least outside-the-box) decisions.

To do that, we have to take personal responsibility for how we live. You're not responsible for past traumas—for the things you can't control or that set you up for failure. You are, though, responsible for how you're going to choose to live your life *moving forward* despite all those factors.

What are the things you need to change to get yourself free enough to dream? Are there factors holding you back that, if you addressed them, would open up your world to a sea of possibilities and to a world of priority-based living? You are not in control of everything that happens in your life, but you are in control of how you respond to those challenges. What do you need to do to get unstuck?

The Big Question: Are You Hurting Your Kids and Your Family by Working or by Living According to Your Priorities?

My enlightened sunrise porch moment brought about a huge revamp for me and my family, but it didn't mean I could or *wanted to* stop working. In fact, I had to work harder during that year to reach my goals. Plus, my work, especially this work writing and talking to moms, is still a huge priority for me. I like working. I see it as a part of my identity. Even as I aim to be intentional with my own children, the kind of work I do away from them is purposeful in its own way and makes a difference in other people's lives. (That's the point of work, by the way, other than making money. If you're working and hating it, go back to my story about examining your priorities.)

Even if I feel all purposeful about the choices I've made about saying yes to work, though, that lingering question of how it was affecting my kids still hung out in the back of my head for a long time after my children came along. The clanging, "you're hurting your kids and your family" lie seems loudest, in my world, whenever it has to do with my kids' school experiences. Of all the places it seems working moms are like a square peg trying to fit into a round hole, forever not able to measure up or be fully present enough, it's at school.

I volunteered in my daughter's kindergarten classroom last fall. I sat squeezed onto one of those little teeny chairs for an hour and a half, cutting out paper strips in orange and yellow for the fall classroom paper chain garlands. I didn't interact with my daughter once and, at the end, I had a major cramp in my hand and a painful kink in my neck.

My daughter, however, remembers it differently, and shared boastfully with her sister around the dinner table that "Mommy spent special time with me today," even adding, "It was the best."

To be honest, I signed up because I felt like I should. The temptation to give into mommy guilt has been stronger than ever since she started elementary school. I'm not really sure how that's possible. Heading back to work after maternity leave was a trial, missing out on zoo dates and library times in the preschool years sometimes got me teary, but elementary school? Things should be easier, it seemed to me as I mentally prepared for the year.

Nope. I was wrong. Now, with the schedule and structure of school life, things seemed somehow more complicated, with way more opportunities to miss something important or to just feel like I was missing out on all of it. At first, I thought it was the constant influx of papers to sign or the fundraising kickoffs that made it so overwhelming, but then it happened. An innocent little message popped onto my mobile screen at 9:00 am on a Wednesday from the app my kid's kindergarten teacher uses to communicate with all the class parents.

"We are going on a farm field trip to pick a pumpkin and have a picnic in the hayloft! This is a special time for you and your kindergartner, so please, please try your very best to be there."

My heart sank. The event, the message said, was a week away. There was absolutely no way I could make it. I had a full panel of patients already lined up and a staff of people depending on me to show up in my pediatrics office. I imagined my daughter sitting alone, crying, eating her boring lunch on some scratchy hay bale, because her mom had to work. I was feeling guilty about how this would make her feel.

Yep, that message made me think pretty hard about just how good a mom I am and what it actually means to be a good mom. It got in my head, making me question, even though I've been on the "it takes a village to raise a child and I'm not the only person in that village" train for as long as I can remember, if I was messing up my kids by not being available to them at all times.

Here's what I realized after soul-searching for a day and a half (listen carefully because this might change your whole worldview like it did for me): *I'm the best mom for my kids not in spite of the fact that I work and have dreams but because I do.*

My kids are watching me all the time. They see me hustling hard to reach my goals and being 100% committed to my vision for myself and for them. No, I'm never going to crochet them intricate Halloween costumes or greet them with homemade cookies in the afternoon, but I am going to give them a shining example of how to contribute to their communities and how to make a difference in the lives of other people. I'm going to show them that the best version of any girl, or of any mom, or of any person, for that matter, is the version that is unapologetically true to herself. Above all, I'm going to be completely invested in my children in the ways that really matter, teaching them the life skills they need to thrive; showing them that women can be nurturers, contributors, and all-out bosses at home and professionally; giving them support, attention, and unconditional love.

If this was not a book for working women, I'm sure someone would write me an email about how all moms are valuable. I could not agree with that more. Maybe you used to love being a stay-at-home mom and you work only because you have to or you work part time. I totally get it. Own that. Working moms aren't better than stay-at-home moms (or vice versa), and mommy guilt doesn't start and stop with work choices—if you didn't know that already, now you do. We all have to resist comparing ourselves to other moms or trying to be something that we're not, no matter how we spend our days. Just like we have to get our priorities in order, we also have to prioritize where and how we spend our time when it comes to mothering.

It doesn't matter that Julie's mommy packs only organic, handmade zucchini muffins each day in her kids' lunches or that Jake's mother volunteers 3 times a week in the classroom but you don't. Maybe your contribution to your kids' lives looks different. In these situations you have to remind yourself about the goals and priorities you set for yourself. You might be a music lover who can teach your kids to embrace life by throwing impromptu dance parties on a Tuesday night. You may work as a customer service agent at a call center and can show your kids how to extend grace and kindness even when others treat you unfairly or get frustrated. You might be an expert business executive who can teach your kids how to negotiate well for themselves, avoiding risky behaviors based on peer pressure down the line. Every working mom has some unique skill or superpower she's imparting to her kids *because she works*, not in spite of it.

ℯↄℯↄℯↄ

CONFESSIONS FROM WORKING MOMS: Marcy runs an independent bookstore. She's teaching her daughter resilience by example. She talks about her professional ups and downs with her 10-year-old daughter, Nina, all the time but always specifically emphasizes how proud she is of her own tenacity.

"In the early days, we barely made enough money to keep the store running. We lived off mac and cheese when Nina was younger because we just couldn't afford anything else. Things were always tight, and I questioned whether the time away from the kids was worth it," Marcy told me.

One day Marcy came home to find Nina baking cookies and selling them in front of her house to bring the neighborhood together and "bring in a little cash."

"At first, I didn't take it too seriously," Marcy said, "but then she told me, 'I think I'm going to sell a bunch if I just keep at it. It's like a real business—we might have to wait a little while people tell their friends to come buy something, but it's worth it. It's just like your store, Mommy.' Wow, that made my heart just burst. She's watching me as a business-woman, and she sees herself in that role too. I'll be happy with whatever she decides to do or to be in her life, but the fact that she sees me and wants to emulate what I'm doing, and that I'm teaching her to stick with hard things by doing it myself—it gave me a lot of encouragement."

ℯↄℯↄℯↄ

Are there moms (working and nonworking, by the way) who let the pendulum swing a little too far (even unwittingly) in the direction of self-prioritization to the detriment of their children? Yes, of course. I'm not giving a green light here on complete DIY mothering without guidance and accountability. I bet, though, that's not you. The vast majority of mothers I meet are on the other end of the spectrum—they're trying so hard to not let their kids or some imaginary vision of perfect motherhood down that they miss out on actually enjoying mom life.

Great moms don't try to be someone else; they try to be themselves. Of course, they provide consistency, and they give focused attention to their children at regular intervals. They also, though, figure out who *they* are and what *they* really need first. That may seem selfish at first, but it's really not. Here's why: your kids are watching you. They want to see you happy and fulfilled. They need to see you living according to your priorities so they can do it too someday. If your children see you wistful and guilty, they'll learn to be that way too. If they see you choosing joy, they'll be more likely to mirror it back.

My daughter attended the farm field trip without a parent. My mom went in my place. Guess what? It wasn't some huge catastrophe. She didn't cry, and she wasn't sad. She adapted. She grew even more resilient. She had a great time and told all her friends, "My mommy couldn't come because she's making sure people don't get polio today" (since I'm a pediatrician), and "My daddy couldn't come because he's helping people walk today" (since he's a physical therapist). When I got home from work, we got out our own gardening tools, listened to *Hamilton* on repeat, and talked about how she planned to be an artist–mathematician–coffee shop owner who sells my book with each latte. We talked about the challenges we both faced that morning and how our positive approaches made a difference in how the day unfolded and how we felt in the end. I couldn't be prouder of her or of us—unapologetically content with our dreams and our household.

You may believe all this as fervently as I do, but it sure helps to have the scientific evidence to back it up (because on my hardest, most guilt-ridden, or just plain tiring days, sometimes my brain gets all fuzzy about what's the truth and what's not). Stewart D. Friedman, practice professor of management at the Wharton School of Business and the former head of the Ford Motor Company Leadership Development Center, wrote about how our careers affect our children in his *Harvard Business Review* recap of his work on the subject. He found no matter how much time parents spent working, children were healthier emotionally when moms *and* dads believed family should be top priority and parents found work enjoyable and stimulating—it was a source of challenge and creativity. Interestingly, moms who enjoyed more control at work (authority and discretion) were also associated with emotionally healthier kids, as were moms who took time for self-care and relaxation.

Friedman's research was fascinating when it comes to high-quality time versus high-quantity time at home. Being at home more versus at work more was not protective if, when moms were home, they spent the time doing household labor. In fact, there were some associations with moms performing high levels of housework during nonwork hours and *increased* behavioral problems. Instead, what mattered most was how present and available moms and dads were to their children, both physically and psychologically, when they weren't working.

Here's the bad news: working moms can't do it all. The good news? They can choose to do a few things really, really well—choosing calm over chaos, prioritization over stress, and intention over busyness. The even better news? Even our kids don't need us to be the ideal mother society fantasizes about, conformed to someone else's expectations. In fact, when we model a more intentional approach, they learn it too. We lead by example so that, even though they may be tempted to overburden themselves with multiple junior high school sports, or with high school cello, debate, and chess club commitments simultaneously, they're free not to. We take away their sense of obligation to keep a hectic schedule by doing the same thing in our own lives.

Our kids don't need us to be around them every moment to be well-adjusted and emotionally stable, either. They just need us to get rid of all the noise and start living based on the things that really matter to us—to start living now based on where we, ultimately, want to end up.

Chapter 4

Why Self-care Is Critical for Working Moms

*Caring for myself is not self-indulgence. It is self-preservation,
and that is an act of political warfare.*

—*Audre Lorde*

A few summers back, I had the ultimate self-care revelation. I took a mommyhood vacation. Well, actually, I worked all week while my kids and husband went on vacation. Even so, without 2 little ones on my heels and in my arms for 5 days, it felt like a holiday getaway. I'd taken way too much time off earlier in the year to care for my kids using my sick days, leaving me short on summer days off from work, so we decided to divide and conquer this time around. While my husband played on the beach with his side of the family and our children, I stayed behind and kept my job.

What I Learned

Of course, I knew I would miss my girls the second they boarded the airplane, but I also knew I had a rare opportunity to do a lot of the things I never get to do, things that never happen because it's hard to coordinate everyone's needs on a weekly basis and because, when my kids are around, I really like to hang out with them.

I went to a movie (it had been 3 years since my last in-theater experience), and I met my girlfriend for game night at her house. I cooked myself breakfast on Sunday morning and sat in silence as I peacefully drank my entire cup of coffee. The midmorning yoga class I loved pre-babies was finally an option. No one called and asked when I would be home. *I was free.* You're probably going to guess my next line, right? "And then you realized you didn't really want to be free." Incorrect. I loved it. The guilt was gone. My time was mine. I could choose. You read the last chapter, right? Freedom is kind of my jam.

My revelation on my mommyhood vacation was more nuanced than that. Here's what I realized: it would not be that hard to replicate any of this in my normal life because—shocker—my life before kids was not that interesting. I like to romanticize it in my mind. I like to pine away for it, but I don't really have to because none of the things I wanted to do without the pull of responsibility were that extravagant. No, I can't do them all in a 48-hour continuous stretch every weekend, but I *can* sprinkle them into a weekly and monthly routine, achieving that same college-era "I just finished finals for the summer and I am free as a bird" feeling—that feeling of no pressure, no obligation, no me-shaped hole in my heart.

It's not that I didn't already make self-care a priority. It's that my attitude, while I was taking care of myself, was often that I was on borrowed time or that my kids were wistfully wishing for me each time I went away for short periods. "What if I could shift that?" I thought. Is it possible to be mindful about the way I parent, about my perspective on the stage of motherhood I'm in, and also about my self-care moments? What if I could truly enjoy my opportunities for enjoyment, sans mom guilt and martyrdom? I realized I didn't have to torture myself. I could just enjoy.

In my pediatrics office, the moms I see who learn that mindset trick are happier and better adjusted to their working mommy roles. They care deeply about their children, but they know that having healthy priorities means not always putting their kids first—sometimes it means consciously, mindfully, putting themselves first for discrete periods of time. On the other hand, the moms I see who never acknowledge their own needs, or who live in a "less than" mentality, struggle more than they need to. Those moms never get to fully enjoy motherhood *or* their own personhood.

When I reunited with my babies at the end of our journeys, I felt complete again—back with the people I loved the most. But I didn't regret the decision we made to let me have some moments by myself. My mommyhood vacation taught me a lot—mostly about how I didn't need more time, I just needed more perspective. I needed to understand the factors that were holding me back from taking care of myself like I need to. In fact, there are 4 key factors that I find keep most moms from prioritizing self-care.

Mommy Guilt

Mommy guilt is real. It's all over the place. When you drop your kids off at child care, when you leave them with the nanny, when you go out on a date—it's there, lurking in the corners, just waiting for you to break down. But why? Did our moms feel this way? Did our grandmas?

Probably not to the same degree we do. We're living in a new world, one where women are competing against men in the workplace and where roles are changing for both men and women. That kind of evolution doesn't happen overnight. It happens incrementally, often with a few steps back as we try to move forward. That adds a lot of pressure for working moms.

Plus, we all have information overload. Given the number of books about parenting out there, the social media advice coming from every angle, the how-to advice from mom groups, it can be daunting to start to trust yourself about what the best way is for you to parent your children and to take care of yourself without feeling like you're letting someone down. Social media apps make it look like every other mom has it all together and that, when you have your kids, you should just follow steps 1, 2, and 3 to make them well-behaved and happy. When they're not, it can lead to disappointment and frustration.

Also, most working moms have had years of adulting before they get around to having kids. I was in my mid-30s when I had my first baby. As a result, I had a great life before my children came around: I traveled, ate good food, had late nights, was already working full time, exercised almost every day, and carved out plenty of moments to decorate my home and relax on the weekends. Set that in contrast to my life as a new mom? It wasn't very appealing. I had complete loss of control. I couldn't go anywhere, and I had no time to myself unless my kids were asleep. When they were awake, anything could happen.

I was used to planning something and having it go the way I wanted it to go. If it didn't, I could call customer service or write a Yelp review and someone would fix it (I've actually never written a Yelp review in my whole life, but you know what I mean). The thing is, there is no Yelp when it comes to your kids and their needs. That sense of control over your world that you thought you had goes away when you have a child, and that can feel devastating.

✂✄✂✄✂✄

CONFESSIONS FROM WORKING MOMS: "When you take your kids out in the baby and toddler years—wherever you take them—you're always rolling the dice," I remember my friend

Nichole telling me when I was pregnant for the first time. "It can go well—everyone with their best manners, the food arrives when they said it would at the restaurant—but, more often than not, it can go terribly wrong—food all over the floor, babies wailing in their high chairs...you have to be ready for both."

Perhaps most real and pressing is the sense of guilt we all feel from our kids themselves. My youngest daughter perfected the "Mommy, don't go" cry when she turned 1 year old. It consisted of, "Mom, mom, mom, mom, mom, mom," over and over again. It reliably happened when I was heading out to my job in the morning or when I was all geared up to work out. It hardly ever happened to my husband (or maybe I just don't notice it). It was enough to make me cry in my car occasionally, especially when my kids were in the throes of separation anxiety.

Separation anxiety can be especially triggering for working moms but is a normal part of childhood development. (For more information, see the "Separation Anxiety" box later in this chapter.) It can present in babies, toddlers, and elementary school kids. All children are different. One child may have extreme separation anxiety as a baby but sail through the toddler years. Other children may be unphased by their moms leaving in the first year after birth but experience more distress during times of separation as they grow older.

I've spent a lot of time thinking through the choices we all have when it comes to responding to mommy guilt. I say "respond" because about 10% of the time I just gut-level react to my kid's sadness at goodbyes, and no amount of frontal lobe, executive functioning can overcome it. I'm assuming the same thing happens to you every once in a while.

The options are simple: give in, or fight back.

Giving in is easier in the short run. It feeds our desire to make sure everyone around us is taken care of, even at our own expense. The problem is that giving in yields horrible

Separation Anxiety

Separation anxiety is a normal part of childhood development that peaks around 10 to 18 months when babies start to understand object permanence (the fact that if something is hidden it still exists) but can be common in toddlers and preschoolers too.

Babies

When a baby has separation anxiety, she's fearful her parent will never return again. She may cry when her mom or dad leaves the room, cling or cry in new situations, or awake at night after she has been consistently sleeping through the night.

Toddlers

Some toddlers have minimal separation anxiety early on but have more difficulties around 15 or 18 months old. Because they're particularly sensitive to hunger and fatigue, they're more likely to have distress if separations occur around mealtimes or sleep times. Toddlers will become tearful, cry loudly, and be persistent when they have separation anxiety.

Preschoolers

Preschoolers may also experience separation anxiety, especially during transitions like starting a new child care. They also, though, understand more clearly how their emotional pleas affect us as parents. Consistency and quick exits during separations is important at this age.

To Help Your Child

- Introduce an object like a blanket or soft toy to make separations easier.
- Avoid prolonging goodbyes.

Separation Anxiety (*continued*)

- Have the sitter distract your baby or child with a toy as you're leaving.

- Be honest: if you walk out of a room and say you'll be back, actually do it.

- Make sure your child is well-fed and well-rested whenever possible before separations.

long-term results. We're less physically and mentally healthy, and it's easier to get irritated and to lose our cool with our kids. But remember, don't lose your balance, stay strong, as you are setting an example that you hope your children will follow in their own lives.

Fighting back is harder in the here and now because it requires the ultimate exercise in trade-offs and benefits. It requires deciding that we're just as important as the other people in our lives and the other obligations we have. It requires facing our deepest fears. Fears like "taking care of myself will in some way damage my children" or "taking care of myself will mean my kids will internalize a message that they don't matter to me" *or* "someone else (grandparents, my partner, my friends) will judge me and think that I'm a bad mom by spending time investing in my (yes, I'm going this far with it) sanity when I already take hours away from my children by working." The truth is, though, time spent taking care of the commitments we all have (including work) and checking off things on our to-do list (like housework or errands) is not the same as time spent doing what actually feeds us as women.

Time

Staying committed to doing the few things we really want to do is difficult. There are so many barriers and so little time. We've all been here: You have a late meeting at work. You have to take your kids to soccer practice or piano lessons. You should be organizing that closet, or those papers, or... name the task. There are a million things that can take precedence over taking care of ourselves, and it can seem like there are not enough hours in the day. Even though taking care of ourselves doesn't have to take hours and hours, it can sometimes be hard to find even 5 minutes to spare.

Chaos

Most days, if I let it, my life would feel pretty much out of my control. I get to work and someone informs me about a newborn I need to see at the hospital the next morning. That sets my wake-up time back from 6:15 am to 5:15 am. My kids wake up unexpectedly in the middle of the night, leaving me even more tired than anticipated at the end of the next day. When I do go out of the house with my kids, or sometimes even when I stay in, who knows what kind of mood they will be in, who will have a meltdown, or what food will end up all over me. You know how it goes. Your eighth grader forgets his permission slip for the field trip and you have to make a 30-minute round-trip detour or your 9-year-old has friend drama that needs time and a listening ear. In the flash of a moment, those 5 minutes you had to spare are gone.

So many working moms tell me they feel like they can barely catch up, much less add something extra to their lives, but that's the entire point of self-care.

● Take a second to regain perspective so we can handle the chaos again.
● Back away from the chaos so we can figure out what's making it so hectic in the first place.

● Examine what we need to change or cut out so we can enjoy our lives more.

● Examine how we can better cope with what we can't change during that season of our lives.

Mama, you don't need a break *despite* the fact there's chaos; you need a break *because* there's so much chaos in your life.

Institutional and Social Bias

Freelance writer Danielle Campoamor rocked the internet with her *Romper* piece, "Moms Would Look After Themselves After Baby If They Could—But It's Impossible Without Help." Listen to what she said about how moms can't take care of themselves well because the world doesn't take care of them.

> We, as a society, tout the importance of taking care of moms in a variety of ways. We laud the benefits of self-care, usually in expensive spa-form. We talk about "putting on your oxygen masks" before you assist others. We hold up the value of "villages" and encourage parents to find or build their own. We celebrate whatever clichéd garbage is written in the Mother Day cards we haphazardly remember to send once a year, along with a gift certificate to a nail salon or overpriced brunch. But rarely, if ever, do people actually take care of the mom in their lives. No, the onus on taking care of a mother falls on the mother herself. She must add "self-care" to her never-ending list of obligations and responsibilities and priorities. And make no mistake, in the year 2019, that list is only getting larger....What I need is someone to actually care for me. To make me food and take my children so I can focus on myself and only myself. I need someone to see all the things I do for everyone else...and *do them for me.*

She's right. The odds are stacked against us when it comes to taking time to focus on ourselves. In a perfect world, our partners and our employers would appreciate the effort we're putting in at work and at home and would take some of that effort on themselves. They would value our contributions and our need for restoration. We would have equality. Someone else would take care of us. I think we can all agree that ideal is worth fighting for.

Don't wait for that elusive day to arrive to take care of yourself, though, because who knows when it will. We miss out on joy in the present moment when we decide we'll be happy only if the world wises up to our needs and rights, sometime in the future. I don't know about you, but I can't wait that long.

I hope our kids and grandbabies don't have the same struggles we do when it comes to convincing the world we're better mothers, workers, and people when we're whole and rested. In fact, I believe they won't. We can decide to care for ourselves even if they won't by choosing to make ourselves a priority despite the world we live in, pushing quality and equity forward in the process.

Why Self-care Is So Critical

Ever notice how, when you take a weekend to unplug or even an hour to relax, you're actually able to accomplish more in the hours or days that follow? Self-care is never a waste. Quite the opposite. When we regroup, relax, or refocus, we're able to offer those who depend on us or who partner with us the very best of ourselves. We can be more present and more peaceful.

You've probably heard the phrase, "You can't pour from an empty cup." It's cute, but author Penny Reid's *Beard in Mind* quote, "Don't set yourself on fire trying to keep other people warm," captures the necessity of self-care for moms much more accurately. It highlights the pain we can put ourselves through unnecessarily. There are no brownie points for motherhood martyrdom. You can't fill other people up, you can't be your best self to the rest of the world (including your children), if you are not doing the things you need to do to be content.

In other areas of your life—physical fitness endeavors, educational training programs, work turmoil—you may be able to muddle through for a short season with no reprieve or reflection, but motherhood is different. Motherhood is a marathon, not a sprint. When I looked at the Ideal versus Reality lists I made with my friend in the last chapter, I thought about how, for a season, I could probably handle having my desires and my actual life be completely upside down but, in the long run, it was really not how I wanted things to be. I also felt angry and disappointed when I thought about how, if I didn't make a change, this could be the way I lived my life for the next 20 years. I realized I would be totally unhealthy mentally and physically, with only a semi-clean house and some angry, maladapted kids to show for all of my efforts.

There are real benefits to consistent self-care. The first—and the most important—is being content with your current life situation. I was driving in the car with my mom and my daughter a few years ago, before the whole aha moment at the beach. *Tangled* was blaring by special request (not mine). Rapunzel belts out, "Tell me, when will my life begin?"

Without even thinking about it, I turned to my mom and said, "Yeah, sheesh, when will it begin?"

She looked over at me, quizzical. "Honey, you're over 35 years old with two kids, a house, and a dog. Your life has not only begun, it is in full swing." Leave it to a cartoon soundtrack to make me stop in my tracks. My life is not sometime in the future, when things are less complicated or easier. It is this exact second. If I don't take care of myself now and set up good habits for the rest of my life (or at least for the foreseeable future in my motherhood experience), it will be all on me if I look back at my "best years" and think, "Well, I certainly missed the point." The same is true for you.

The second benefit of self-care is for your partner. This is sometimes one of the hardest, least discussed areas of dual-career families, especially if you live with someone who is at first resistant to the idea of you taking "extra" time away from your kids, but I am not on a crusade for you to be the only one in your household who takes care of herself. If you have a partner, that person *also* needs time to explore his or her passions, to connect with himself or herself, and to recharge.

Don't forget, self-care may look different for your partner than it does for you. Maybe your partner's version of self-care is a beer with a friend at a soccer game, not time saying "om" in yoga class. Just because it doesn't seem super spiritual or deep, don't judge. Self-care is not ever about the activity itself; it is about the intention behind it. Whatever it is, it makes you happy, and you feel restored afterward.

Make a Self-care Plan

The only way to take the best care of your family is to make sure you're taking time to take care of yourself. Can you push through and be a mommy martyr for the next 18 years? Sure. Will it leave you resentful and angry? Most definitely. Not all self-care is about setting goals. In fact, most of self-care is just about consistently looking inward at what's working well and where you feel stuck. In the next chapter, we'll talk more about creating the kind of consistent self-care ritual and routine that provides consistent opportunities for reconnecting to the things that really matter to you. Every once in a while, though, in seasons when things become incredibly stymied and need to change, like they did for me, you're going to want to set some goals.

I'll admit it feels awkward at first to talk about "self-care goals." When I think of goal-setting exercises, I first think of a corporate boardroom with a bunch of high-level bosses sitting around in high-backed chairs. Most moms I know think about self-care as a series of discrete activities or about a simple routine like we talked about earlier on. They don't consider self-care in terms of goal setting. Self-care is usually much more fluid, much more emotional, much more about filling needs in the moment.

But, sometimes, goal setting applies perfectly to self-care. It takes getting down to brass tacks when you really want to make a change in your life and you're not sure how to do it. If your Ideal List looks nothing like your Reality List, that means it's time to dream a little bigger and look a little deeper. If, for example, high on your Ideal List is spending time pursuing your passions, things you used to spend time on before you had kids (like going back to school, starting a small business, or building a more connected social village), then you're going to want to do it in a more structured way. That's where SMART goals, described by George Doran in the eighties, come in: specific, measurable, attainable, realistic, and time bound.

SMART Goals

Specific
Make sure you have a concrete goal in mind. "I want to feel better about myself" is not a goal. It's a great reflection. It's a starting place, but it's just too ambiguous. There is no way to tell if you've actually achieved your goal once you get there.

Example: "I will talk to my best friend on the phone once a week" is concrete.

Measurable
Measurable goals have an outcome you can assess after a certain amount of time to determine your level of progress. That way, you know when you've met your goal and can set a new goal.

Example: "I want more joy" is not a goal. What does "more joy" look like? Instead, "I will complete

(continued)

SMART Goals (*continued*)

5 minutes of peaceful journaling per day" is more measurable.

Attainable

If you set a goal that is too far out of reach, the chances of you reaching that goal are pretty slim. Instead, set a goal that is possible to reach.

Example: an unattainable goal for me would be, "I will be a marathon runner next month." Instead, break it down a bit more; "I will complete a 10-km run in 3 months" is more likely.

Realistic

Realistic goals are goals that are not based in fantasy. Instead, they are possible to achieve, even if it takes multiple, painful steps to get there.

Example: "I will go to a 5-week yoga retreat in Italy by the end of next week" is never going to happen. Try, "I will sign up for a virtual health retreat by the end of next week."

Time Bound

Even with self-care goals, time is an important element. Give yourself a concrete end point for your goal. How long will you give yourself to make it happen?

Example: "My goal is to consistently exercise 5 times a week for 30 minutes at a time by 3 months from now. I'll decide on an exercise activity by 1 week from now, I'll determine my child care needs by 2 weeks from now, and I'll purchase any fitness equip-ment I need to complete my workouts by 1 month from now to work toward that goal."

When I stared into the ocean on that balcony with my daughter, imagining my life as I really wanted it, I had a specific dream: I have freedom. For me, at that moment, that meant financial freedom. That dream was tied to other deeper, significantly more important dreams, like, "I have as much time as I want to spend with my family," and "I help other moms win at parenting without losing themselves." Those dreams were the "why" behind this first dream, but I knew I had to get financially fit if I ever wanted to have the bandwidth to make those other dreams a priority. My first goal associated with my financial freedom dream was, "I am debt-free with no student loan or personal credit card obligations." Accordingly, I started making plans to reach that goal, like changing my living situation and my spending habits.

"You have to know where you're going, and you have to know your why," says author and speaker Rachel Hollis in her book, *Girl, Stop Apologizing.* "For those of you who start and stop, start and stop, start and stop, if you've gone off your resolution fifty times before, it's because your why wasn't strong enough…You have to have the leverage — you have to know your why — or you will never make change. You have to know what to focus on, or you will never make progress."

෪෨෪෨

Self-care gets a bad rap, especially when we start acting like it's something that's fully in our control, something we could do better if we just tried a little harder or spent a little more money. It also gets misinterpreted, seen as an activity to complete or a task to check off. At its heart, though, self-care is just that: making sure we take good care of ourselves (in big, action-item, reach-a-new-goal kinds of ways and in teeny-tiny, change-the-way-we-think-about-ourselves-and-our-lives kinds of ways) so we can take great care of everything else without resentment and regret. It's a mindset shift, a perspective change. It's about establishing consistent ways to cope with the pressures and demands that face us every day, about thinking beyond today to the bigger picture, about realizing how the ways we spend our moments ultimately end up defining our lives.

Chapter 5

Choosing a Self-care Ritual and Routine

When you recover or discover something that nourishes your soul and brings joy, care enough about yourself to make room for it in your life.

— Jean Shinoda Bolen

CONFESSIONS FROM WORKING MOMS: My friend Jenny is a go-getter. She likes lists and agendas. She thrives on structure. She's a planner, especially when she's not making sales and retaining accounts at her marketing firm. When she's not at work, sometimes she feels restless. "When I have a day to myself (which I hardly ever have), I find myself overplanning it, making an itinerary for myself even if I don't have to."

My Itinerary

8:00 am	Take the kids to school.
8:05 am	Coffee with a good book
9:15 am	Leave in time for jog with friend. Make kids' haircut appointment.
12:00 pm	Meeting with air conditioning contractor at the house
1:00 pm	Doctor's appointment
2:15 pm	Quick grocery store run for upcoming trip
3:00 pm	Pick up kids at school.

3:30 pm	Luke to soccer practice
4:00 pm	Rebecca to piano
5:00 pm	What's for dinner? Did I thaw the meat?

"By 5:00 pm I'm exhausted. I'm realizing that I'm just as type A about my self-care as I am about my job. I have this uncanny way of making things that are supposed to be relaxing and enjoyable a total drain." Jenny, like many moms, has a tendency to make self-care yet another chore instead of a much-deserved reset.

In this chapter, we're going to talk specifically about how to create self-care rituals and routines. We'll walk our way through setting up specific plans to make self-care happen and to reach our goals, but, before we do it, we have to address this simple truth: self-care is not self-care if it's making us more stressed or feeding our penchant for perfectionism. Self-care is about finding ways to make sure, as we're working, and parenting, and doing all the "stuff" of life, that we fit in opportunities to actually live it—that we make time for the things that make us truly joyful, not just at the end of our working mom journeys but also along the way there. I'm not talking about epic trips and exotic adventures here, I'm talking about the little things that make us feel alive. In fact, some of the least mind-blowing, least perfect experiences can make us feel the most whole.

This past holiday season, my 6-year-old daughter reminded me just how important it is to be OK with less than perfect, even in the self-care arena. See, apparently the holiday was a major bust for her.

"Mom, I think I don't really want to celebrate Christmas again," she told me December 26 at 8:00 am. Her little body let out a heavy sigh, and her long lashes turned down to the floor.

"Why's that, sweetie?"

"Well, it wasn't snowing, so we didn't have a white Christmas, and some of my gifts weren't what I told Santa that I wanted. So, we might as well not celebrate the holiday next year."

Now it was my turn to breathe a big sigh. I know you know exactly why. I spent weeks making a list and checking it twice (no, 3 times) to make sure everyone was fully accounted for in the Santa department and, knowing my oldest is especially sensitive, I made sure to go over her part of the list a few times just to ward off disappointment. This is not the first time I've heard about a birthday or even a school day that is less than ideal. Despite my best efforts, though (and things way out of my control, like the weather, for instance), I guess Christmas didn't meet the mark in her book.

"Darling," I told her, "you get what you get, and you don't throw a fit. Santa and Mommy can't read your mind, but we love you very much and wanted Christmas to be special. I bet you loved the chocolate cake you got at dinner and the sparkly chandelier you got for your room." Yes, you heard that right. I bought my kid a crystal (plastic), fancy (clearance special) light fixture as a present. The moment she opened the package, her eyes lit up like she'd just won the lottery.

Her eyes sparkled again at the memory, and she reluctantly acquiesced to the idea that we would not be doing a second-chance holiday extravaganza to make up for any failures in the first round. I was at peace with her disappointment and, after some coaching, so was she.

It's pretty easy for me to help my children through their disappointments when they're unreasonable — to brush them off as immaturity. It's harder, though, when it comes to my own expectations and threshold for disappointment — not so much at the holidays, but for my life as a whole.

I realized as I watched my daughter sulking that I have a way of sulking a lot too—of really needing certain aspects of my world to be just the way I want them to be…or I consider them not good at all. Sound like you too?

In fact, I remember crying on the couch a few years ago about that very thing. I was complaining to my husband about how I never actually get to a spin class, or a yoga class or a _____ (fill in the blank with a walk, or a jog, or an online exercise class), with everything on my plate. There I was, getting all teary with my husband about how I can never fit a workout in, about how I feel some days like physical fitness is a totally wasted goal now that my post-2-baby, late-30s bod takes about 150% more effort to maintain, much less improve. I kept extrapolating past fitness to the bigger picture—to the picture almost every mom I know paints sometimes about wanting just a few moments of freedom to reconnect to herself.

My husband sat next to me on the couch. He hates analyzing for the sake of analysis but has a way of speaking streamlined wisdom in the moments that really count. After offering up alternatives to my preconceived self-care plans (eg, take a run when you get home with 1 of the kids, get a pass to the tiny gym on the first floor of your building and jump on the elliptical for 15 minutes at lunch, squeeze in 10 minutes on an exercise video), all of which I turned down, he said this:

"You know, it doesn't have to be perfect to be great."

He was so right. Sometimes we make things—even good things that are meant to be relaxing and rejuvenating—so much more complicated than they need to be. Just like we try to teach our own kids to be flexible problem solvers, we have to do the same thing ourselves.

Wondering how this story ends? I took his advice, and I was happier for it. I started running again, something I've enjoyed since junior high school but have done way less of in the last 5 years. It's like I'm saying "hi" to an old friend. I do a lot of at-home online high-intensity interval training work-outs in my basement. I still make it to classes when I can, but the pressure is off to make it all work in quite the same way. The added benefit? I've started taking my kids with me—my oldest riding right alongside me or my youngest riding in the stroller—and it's giving us even more quality time together.

Talking about making plans and trying to find ways to stick to them may feel a bit prescriptive, a little oversim-plified. That's because it is. Reaching dreams, setting goals, even making small plans are important, but, in the end, our success in achieving what we set out to do is never under our complete control. Life gets in the way. Finances get in the way. Physical illness gets in the way. As much as I wish we could all strap on those hiking boots and climb every moun-tain without planning ahead for a potential storm or even a "Path closed today. Do not enter." sign, that approach would be foolhardy.

Does that mean we just throw in the towel, deciding to let the winds take us where they will? Absolutely not. It means we set out a course based on our priorities, we set up sys-tems that are the most likely to get us where we want to go, and then we stay flexible and resilient in the face of obstacles that momentarily derail us and catastrophes that completely throw us off track.

Finding a Self-care Ritual That Works for You

Even if over the years I've learned to be more flexible and cognizant that I'm ultimately a tiny ant on a big, huge, spin-ning planet—*one I'm not spinning*—I'm still determined to help myself and other moms find ways to manage the chaos. Even if we're not in complete control of the world or of our lives, we are absolutely, 100% (please listen because I am going to say this with italics so it will stand out to you) *in control of the way we respond to the world around us, the way we show up for ourselves and our families. We're in control of the way we choose to spend our efforts and time.* That means that we're in control of choosing to take moments—and sometimes hours—specifically for ourselves.

Even more important, my self-care ritual is based on specific goals I have, and my less-than-perfect plan works for me now because, for at least a while, I got a little regimented. Even now, as I make concessions on what type of self-care I do throughout the week or where I go to make it happen, I still make sure I thought through what worked for me and what didn't. I tried things out. I reevaluated and then started again. If you're a self-care novice, if the thought of incorporating self-care into your day-to-day life sounds incredibly daunting, start here.

Decide You're Worth 5 Minutes a Day

When you wake up in the morning, you are starting fresh on your journey toward social-emotional health for you and your family. You have a chance to renew your commitment to your dreams and your priorities. Take it. Decide you're worth 5 minutes a day thinking about the things you're grateful for, visualizing who you want to be, and remembering what your priorities are. If you're inching toward a dream, use that time to think about the goal you're working on to get there. As you move through your day, all kinds of distractions and barriers are going to come up, so find 5 minutes early on to get intentional about what really matters to you.

This does not have to be formal, though there are about a billion goal-setting and intention-setting journal systems out there for sale. If it helps you to focus to write it all out like it does for me, by all means get your pencil sharpened. You could use your 5 minutes alone in the shower to do this, or take 5 minutes in the car on the way to work to move through this process. When I have early morning meetings, I use the microphone feature on my phone to record my

5-minute sessions. The point is to take the time to remember why you do what you do.

Decide on a Schedule That Fits Your Life

As you develop a self-care plan, you'll have to decide how much time you're willing or able to commit to on a weekly basis. I decided pretty early on that 1 to 2 hours 3 days a week was a reasonable goal.

What is something you can do about every other day, almost every single week? Of course, you will have setbacks like the ones I just described, but if you can commit to 3 times a week most weeks, it will be often enough that you stick with it, and it will become a routine. If you can get to your activity more often, awesome, but 3 times a week is a great start.

I schedule my self-care this way.

1. One weekend morning
2. One weekday evening when my husband is with our kids
3. One weekday evening when a caregiver is with our kids

This is a guideline, something to come back to when life gets in the way and you have not taken good care of yourself in a good long while or when you're first starting out. I'll be honest. I have weeks when none of these 3 days happens. There are days I have to squeeze time in for myself at the very end of the day. I come back to this schedule time and time again. However, this is not about checking off boxes. This is about thinking about how much time you're willing to *give yourself* and what you would do with that time if you had it.

Start With Exercise

If there was going to be 1 single activity that is worth time by yourself and for yourself, physical fitness (if you choose the right activity—anything with an endorphin release) or meditation takes the cake. Physical fitness can give you the chance to deepen your social connections, be mindful, work on your own physical fitness, and set goals for yourself. Meditation also checks many of those same boxes, but there is something valuable in moving our bodies as a way to clear the mental and physical cobwebs away.

This is not about fitting into your favorite jeans (though, obviously, if you're working out consistently you're also likely going to reap the physical benefits). This is also not about spending hours at the gym. This is about finding even 20 minutes on our busiest days to make time for movement so we can reduce stress, clear our minds, sleep better, and release endorphins. We'll talk about building consistent routines in a second, but let's be real: sometimes squeezing in a quick jog around the neighborhood or walking to the grocery store instead of driving is going to have to cut it.

When you do choose a routine, devise one that works for you, not that fits others' expectations or sounds good to everyone else. This is not about them; it's 180% about you.

When I was choosing an exercise program for myself postpartum, my friends and my husband talked a lot about running, Pilates, or joining a gym. Those can be *great* for some people. I have done a lot of running in the past, and it was amazing, but I didn't feel it was the right thing for me this time around.

They also suggested working out first thing in the morning. "Get up really early, go work out, get ready, and then go straight to work," they said.

I tried that for a long time, feeling as if that was the most responsible path to take, the way that would least inconvenience everyone else around me. But it didn't work for 3 reasons.

1. **I never worked as hard as I would later in the day when I went to morning classes.** I felt sorry for myself that I was up so early and didn't push myself because I was proud of myself just for showing up.

2. **I hardly ever actually went.** I always found an excuse—namely, sleeping in as much as possible—but also kids waking up early needing my attention, work meetings, and illness. You name it, I used it as an excuse.

3. **I was exhausted by the time I finished exercising, getting ready for the day, and getting myself to my job.**

I'm sure you can guess how often I worked out. That's right: never. Nope. Self-care is just like birth control. The type of birth control that is best for you is the one you will use consistently. The type of self-care you choose is the kind that fits you and your desires and life.

Instead, I took classes directly after work when I needed the most stress relief. I changed before leaving the office and drove straight to the exercise studio. That way, I didn't lose motivation and was already dressed by the time class started at 6:00 pm.

Almost hilariously, running, early morning online workout videos, and 6:00 am workouts are now the mainstay of my exercise and self-care regimen. That's because I have children who sleep through the night consistently, and I have a lot of early evening work commitments. I try to go to bed by 9:30 pm so that I get a full night's rest by the time I wake up at 5:30 am. I sign up for exercise classes on my studio's app. They have a strict cancellation policy, making it impossible to cancel past 10:00 pm the night before without paying a fine. The threat of a $15 penalty motivates me to show up on time.

Most important, I've learned to give myself some grace. I'm much more concerned with getting some type of physical fitness in consistently than with making sure I work my absolute hardest during every workout session. A different season in my life equals a different self-care approach.

Make It a Multitasker

Three hours a week for 1 to 2 hours is really not much. It makes sense to bundle your benefits so that you get the most bang for your buck from the activity you choose. Look back at your priority list—is there something you can do that accomplishes multiple goals for you? Here are some examples.

- **Group exercise class**—stress relief, physical fitness, mindfulness, camaraderie, alone time to and from the activity
- **A walk around the neighborhood**—fresh air, visual change of pace, physical fitness, mindfulness, maybe an errand or two
- **Virtual hangout with a friend**—building community and support, stress relief, good food

Purposefully Waste Time

CONFESSIONS FROM WORKING MOMS: Samantha, who brings her kids to my pediatrics clinic, craves rest. Her parents emigrated to the United States when she was 3, and, as soon as she was able, she worked in their neighborhood grocery store alongside them.

"I can't remember a time I wasn't working. Through high school, in community college, even now. Working is what I do."

Samantha has a job as a dental hygienist, but it's not enough to pay for everything her 3 kids need. Her oldest daughter seems to grow out of clothes as soon as she buys them, and groceries go quickly in her house. Samantha started asking her boss for some extra administrative tasks around the office so she could earn a little extra. That meant weekends were filled with more and more work.

"At the end of the day, I know my family is home waiting for me to jump into helping them and being 'mom,' but I need a second to decompress. I sit in my car, recline my seat, and take 5 minutes to do absolutely nothing. I need that 'me time' if I'm going to keep on giving to everyone and everything else around me."

CONFESSIONS FROM WORKING MOMS: Lisa is a high-powered surgeon in New York City. We met in medical school. She handles some of the most complicated cancer cases in the country. She's a mom of 2 kids—1 she had just before starting medical school 15 years ago and 1 she had just before starting her 3-year residency training program. She has a lot of stress—or at least a lot of opportunities for stress. I love what she has to say about how she works self-care into her day: "I find at least 20 minutes per day to just waste time, to do something purposefully unproductive."

Let me be clear: being a go-getter is nothing to be ashamed of. I am a tried-and-true, work-my-tail-to-the-bone, stay-up-all-night-'til-the-book-is-finished kind of girl. It's in my blood. That drive and work ethic got me through medical school and led me to triple time it when I developed an online resource for women at Modern Mommy Doc (https://www.modernmommydoc.com) while I raised 2 small children and worked full time as a pediatrician. It took steely determination to get all that done, and it also took a lot of focused hours of working. I wouldn't trade in all that working even if I could because it got me to where I am today. This is not about slacking off; this is about pacing yourself.

"I choose having lunch with a colleague in the park when the weather is good as opposed to sitting at my desk working on charting patient progress notes," Lisa says. "I walk to work instead of taking the cab my company pays for—even if it takes more time to get there. Not every part of my life is rosy and happy. I deal with a lot of disappointment and anger at my job. I've found that I just can't take care of the other people in my life—my kids, my husband, my patients—well if I am running from thing to thing, never enjoying, never seeing life for what it is: fleeting moments that I can never get back. I have to take the time to enjoy life when I can if I want to enjoy life at all."

Maybe you don't have the type of hectic life Lisa does all the time, but I'm sure you have hectic moments. Maybe you don't work 2 jobs like Samantha, but I know you have exhausting days. We all do. If you have a baby or a toddler, sometimes it pays to take advantage of naps and time in the car to get things accomplished, but sometimes it's even better to just *enjoy* versus multitask during "free time." Take a moment—even if it's just 5 minutes—to refocus in the middle of the day.

Choose enjoyment over productivity whenever you can. During both of my maternity leaves, my husband and I were intentional in the early days to watch a lot of comedies and to listen to a lot of frivolously entertaining audiobooks. Once I returned to work, I made it a point *to not* listen to the news on my way home from work. Instead, I used that time to turn on my music, turn it up loud, and enjoy it. I saved my news and podcast consumption for errands and my to-work commute. Now that my kids are a little older, my workdays are still so much more enjoyable (and productive) when I decide to turn off my phone, shut down my computer, and take a second to be with myself or with my colleagues during downtime.

Plan Ahead to Handle Barriers

Whether you've been a mom for 1 minute or 1 decade, you know this: self-care does not happen in a bubble, impervious to real-life factors around us like illness, hiccups in sched-uling, and last-minute interruptions. When I wrote the first draft of this chapter, I was sitting in a beautiful bed-and-breakfast king-size bed on what was meant to be a romantic getaway with my husband. Turns out the stomach flu had a particular interest in attacking my entire family on that exact day. I spent the first 30 hours of the "vacation" making multiple trips to the deluxe bathroom. I never enjoyed the spa jetted tub, but the toilet and I became close friends. Not to fill you in on all the gory details, but let's just say my self-care plans were more than thwarted.

Not every attempt to find balance is quite so viciously attacked by life's forces, but, let's face it, we can use all the help we can get to avoid mishaps along the way and to minimize hassle for ourselves and for everyone around us. I make my self-care rituals work for me by doing 3 things in advance.

Avoiding Stressful Extras or Add-ons

When my first daughter was born, I really could not wait to get out of the house. She was colicky and exhausting, and, in turn, I was a hot mess. It was obvious that I needed a bit of time away from her, but I felt guilty about it, so instead of using minutes and hours away from her to actually spend time on self-care, I spent time doing chores. It helped me feel like I was accomplishing something, like there was a reason beyond self-preservation for getting out and away. Unfortunately, my plan of cramming a bunch of tasks into each free hour I had quickly backfired. Instead of feeling relaxed and ready to parent when I returned home, I felt like the family servant. I did all the work when I was at home with her, when I was at work, *and* when I was away from her in my "spare time."

I'm not alone in filling up hours away from my kids with to-dos, obligations, and tasks. I see moms every day in my office weighed down by the items on their lists, by the checkboxes that have yet to be checked for the day. Sometimes you feel like you're on top of the world when you run a ton of errands all in 1 day so you can feel accomplished

Colic

What It Is

Frequent, prolonged or intense crying or fussiness in an otherwise healthy baby.

- Crying for 3 or more hours a day, 3 or more days a week, for 3 or more weeks.
- Peaks at about 3 hours a day by 6 weeks, declines 1 to 2 hours a day by 3 to 4 months.

What to Do About It

Recreate a womb-like experience—white noise, combined with rocking, swaddling, and using a pacifier, can help to soothe your newborn.

Find a lactation specialist if you're breastfeeding to ensure overfeeding, underfeeding, or sensitivity to potentially irritating foods you're consuming (like milk products, caffeine, or onions) aren't contributing factors.

Take care of yourself. Leave your baby with someone else if you're feeling overwhelmed, angry, or depressed. Postpartum depression and anxiety are common, serious mental health disorders. Reach out for help to your child's pediatrician or your own health care professional if you're struggling.

Talk to your pediatrician—sometimes colic has no cause or treatment, but your pediatrician can help to make sure there is no underlying medical condition causing the baby's discomfort.

and, because, sometimes things just need to get done. But sometimes, you feel run down and even more stressed after running around like a chicken with its head cut off. Instead, pick some times for you that are only about taking care of yourself so you can come home refreshed.

Planning Ahead for Potential Barriers

What are the things you *already* know will make it so your
plan for self-care won't work? How are you going to deal with
them? Instead of pretending like everything will always work
out, make backup plans whenever possible. Make sure that,
for the days something *really* important is on your calendar—
a special date night with your partner, an inspirational conference you've been wanting to attend—you have your most
reliable caregiver set up.

My mom, bless her heart, has not always been the time-
liest. In my early parenting days, if I had an appointment
that required me to be somewhere at an exact time, I either
told her to come 15 minutes earlier than I needed her to be
there or I picked someone else to watch my kids. She's much
better now, but, for a while, it took planning to make sure my
plans were executed well. My husband, bless him too, gets
frustrated when I leave early on a Saturday morning to go to
a class or to meet up with a friend. In the beginning of our
parenting journey, that made me resentful, but now I see it
as a reflection of his desire for early weekend family coziness
after a hectic week.

Now, I plan to attend classes or connect with girlfriends
later in the afternoon after we've had our family morning
time to be together. I also pick opportunities to stack self-
care onto times I'm already out and about (for work or for
meetings) instead of leaving, then coming back, then leaving
again. It's less disruptive to my kids to have larger chunks
of time apart than it is to have the constant emotional tug-
of-war associated with me leaving, then reconnecting, then
leaving again.

Your kids might not be as sensitive as my little ones are.
You may have very punctual parents. Your partner may not
get as hung up on weekend morning traditions as mine, but
I bet you have other factors that threaten to ruin all your
plans, and I *bet* your kids and partner have needs you have

to accommodate when it comes to self-care. Listen to those needs, but don't let them stop you from taking care of yourself. Instead, analyze the real, underlying issue (ie, I feel like a bad mom when I take time for myself) and address it head-on.

Learning How to Filter

Perhaps the best skill you can learn as a working mom is how to filter through society's noise, false messages, and to-dos. I remembered the importance of filtering this last week. I was sitting on my yoga mat at home, eyes closed, trying to breathe. The lights were dim, the music was just right, the online video instructor's voice was calm and melodic as she guided the class in getting centered and getting comfortable, but I just couldn't seem to focus. It's a shame, really, given that I spent all week arranging for that 1 hour—paying extra for my sitter to take my youngest for an hour, timing a business meeting to start directly after I was done, even putting off more "important" errands in the name of self-care.

Yet, somehow, my mind kept flitting in and out of focus despite multiple attempts to bring myself back to the present moment. I was already onto the rest of the day in my head, and somehow also back to yesterday, where I was analyzing an in-office interaction and questioning my clinical decision-making process on a patient's particularly tough condition. Yep, my filter system was broken.

The day's exercise session was a loss. So what? As I took a shower after the class and got back to the rest of my life, I thought about the bigger picture—about what the class represented, about how many of my self-care attempts are affected by my ability to properly filter. I thought about how much time we all waste, especially as mothers, unable to get past the noise, the false messages, and the endless, meaningless to-dos that face us every day. About how, if self-care really is about trying to achieve some type of balance, it's our filter system that—9 times out of 10—keeps us from actually getting anywhere with our attempts.

Filtering Out the Noise

How much time do you spend on your phone? I'm not judging, I'm just asking, because I often have to spend *a lot* of time on my phone (mostly because of the nature of running a blog and a business and promoting both on social media), and I notice that, when I'm on it without a specific task in mind and without a plan to get off of it as fast as possible, my whole life ends up filled with noise.

I follow a link on the internet to a story and it leads me to some other worthless distraction; I scroll through social media and I get sucked into watching some viral video; I hang out online and get bogged down in pictures of professionally decorated homes that I can't afford. It's all noise, and it eats away at the precious moments I do have to actually do what feeds me, what restores me, and what builds me up.

What can we do to get rid of some of the static that clogs our thinking and takes all our time away? I'm guessing you're probably not going to throw your phone into a pool anytime soon, but what if you worked on consciously setting aside times for yourself throughout the week without any devices, even if it was only 20 minutes at a time? What if you purposefully put your phone in a drawer for an hour or 2? What if you minimized the way you used your phone sometimes instead of maximizing it? When we unplug, we leave more space for productivity and for connection—either with ourselves or with other people.

Filtering Out the False Messages

The idea that you matter less than anyone else in your life is a false message, one so many of us buy into day after day. Why is it so hard for us to take good care of ourselves when we become moms? In part, because it feels selfish and indulgent. Because it feels like there are a million other things that we could be doing with our time that would be more productive for our families or would be more helpful to someone else. Because, when we become mothers, we are often seen primarily as caregivers and secondarily as human beings with basic needs. Each time we have a choice to take care of ourselves, we also have an opportunity to choose what messages we'll believe about ourselves and about our place in this world. We have a chance to choose truths over falsehoods.

Filtering Out the To-dos

All those to-dos for my family, myself, and my work that keep piling up in my head? Yeah, I could do without those. Moms who focus solely on getting things done miss out on *life*, plain and simple. Instead, think about how to lessen your load. If you have a partner, figure out a plan for dividing responsibilities along strength lines. No matter what your family construct, stop doing everything for everyone else. Get other people on your team, including your kids. Coaching kids to help with household tasks in an age-appropriate way builds your family community, teaches responsibility, and helps kids develop resilience. Let go of the tasks that don't matter, and give away the tasks that drag you down. You only have the time and the bandwidth to do so much—use the time you do have to narrow in on your priorities.

Chore List by Age	
Age	**Ways to Contribute**
2–3 Years Old	Pick up toys. Put dirty clothes in hamper. Make the bed. Help feed pets.
4–6 Years Old	Pick up toys. Put dirty clothes in hamper. Make the bed. Dust.

Chore List by Age (*continued*)	
Age	**Ways to Contribute**
4–6 Years Old (*continued*)	Wipe up spills. Prepare basic snacks. Put away groceries. Water houseplants. Set and clear table. Help fold laundry.
6–8 Years Old	Make bed. Clean room. Fold laundry. Vacuum. Match clean socks. Unload indoor trash cans. Weed garden. Load and unload dishwasher. Replace toilet paper rolls. Rake leaves.
9–12 Years Old	Make bed. Clean and clear room. Dust, sweep, and clean surfaces. Clean bathroom and sinks. Rake leaves. Walk dogs. Make own snacks and a simple meal. Mow lawn. Bring in mail.
13–18 Years Old	Clean rooms. Supervise younger sibling's chores. Mop floors. Shop for groceries using a list. Do laundry. Wash windows. Prepare food independently. Trim hedges. Clean and maintain yard or garage. Wash and vacuum car.

Getting Realistic: Being OK With the Stage of Motherhood You're in Now and About What That Means for Your Self-care

If you're reading this while holding your newborn and feeling like, "I can barely take a quick shower, let alone plan out a priority list for myself," remember—there is a season. Even though it's tempting to wish away this moment, to hurry ahead to more balance, you may just need to be still for now. Your priorities and your bandwidth may change as your kids grow and your work demands change. What seemed impossible to me as a new mom is a daily part of my life now that my kids are a little older. It's just a fact that our self-care options may change depending on the stage of motherhood we're in, and that's perfectly OK.

It's so normal to wish away the painful parts of parenting. There are plenty of precious moments at each stage of parenthood, but there are also plenty more moments of pure stress and strife. The real danger isn't just with wishing the nasty or all-consuming parts away. It's with these 2 common missteps: trying to fix every natural developmental stage our child goes through and expecting the transition through those stages to progress in a straight line instead of a messy zigzag.

Parenting from a "fix-it" mentality is a trap every parent falls into from time to time. I see it a lot in my practice. Although a lot of new parents understand pretty quickly that feeding troubles and sleepless nights are just part of the game, many have difficulty as each developmental stage (and headache) arises. They look for solutions to problems that can't be fixed, that have to just be waited out. And, although I'm impressed by their tenacious desire and willingness to problem solve, sometimes I think they've been misled along the way by their friends and by society.

No one tells them this crucial parenting pearl: yes, we can prevent and address a lot of health issues that come up for newborns and young kids, but some things (like cluster feeding, sleep regressions, and colic) are more about muddling through with the right perspective than they are about finding quick-fix solutions. Some things just take time to get better. Major caveat here: if you have a serious health concern about your child and are worried about his or her safety or about potential illness, contact your doctor right away.

We also struggle with setbacks and regressions. When an elementary school child seems to be more and more even-keeled, then has a period of heightened emotions and tantrums akin to the early toddler years, we tend to get immediately stressed. When a child has been sleeping through the night for an extended period, then suddenly has a season of sleep regression, it can feel like a major step back. It's hard to wait for the mini storms and developmental detours of childhood to pass without rushing in to make adjustments. We forget that child development and the parenting experience do not move smoothly along a set curve. Often kids take 1 step backward before they catapult forward emotionally, physically, and cognitively. Because it's unpredictable, parenting can be extremely difficult.

Please don't misunderstand me. There are amazing, chart-topping experiences sprinkled between the pain points. Like last night, when my eldest scampered up the stairs to sit through her baby sister's bedtime story and song, crooning right alongside me to "Good Night My Someone," my husband grinning as the 2 shared a hug and a kiss. I tried my hardest to seal our fleeting seconds of peace into my memory, onto my parenting balance sheet.

So why is it so hard for us to be OK with the place we are in our motherhood journeys?

The more I struggle in my own house and watch others do the same, the more clearly I see the true reason. The rest of our lives, on the surface, have some semblance of controllability. All of our 2-hour grocery delivery options and pickup dry-cleaning services trick us into thinking that, if we just complain to the right customer service agent or do the right internet search, we can fix almost anything. Resolution is an easy click away. When we look deeper, though, nothing could be further from the truth when it comes to the challenges of nonconsumer life.

There are seasons. Seasons of struggle. Seasons of celebration. Seasons of muddling through. And seasons of letting it ride—just being OK with the stage of motherhood we're in now.

༄༅༄༅

Once I started writing this book, I realized how many moms are like me—sometimes making self-care work perfectly but usually veering a little too far toward work, then self-correcting too much, overcompensating, finally landing somewhere in the middle again. The cycle continues and, it turns out, that's life. Self-care isn't about being completely regimented. It's about self-reflecting and self-correcting, being aware of how the ways we choose to live our lives work for us or against us.

My wish for you, as you think about ways to incorporate self-care into your own life, is that you'll see self-care as a reflection of motherhood in general—a chance to approach our experiences—with all the ups and downs and unexpecteds that come with them—with the perspective that perfect would be nice but that less than perfect can be pretty amazing too. I hope you'll see that self-care is about continually reevaluating what needs to give a little and what needs to be shored up a little, about prioritizing the right things, then realizing that life sometimes gets in the way of even the best-intentioned priorities.

Chapter 6

Going Back to Work With a New Baby

What's my favorite thing about being a working mom?
Getting to eat lunch and pee as I please!

—Karen, working mom of 3

*W*orking mom Olivia works from home for a mortgage company. She commuted to a traditional office setting before the COVID-19 (coronavirus disease 2019) pandemic, but now her whole team works remotely. She has more flexibility and less time driving in the car, and she feels like life is in balance. She's not sure how she'll do it with a new baby, though. She can't imagine adding a 3-month-old to her already busy workday.

Working mom Stephanie isn't afraid to ask for what she wants or to get what she needs. She works as an attorney for an environmental law firm. She's never been intimidated by much. When she became a new mom, though, she felt unsure as she tried to navigate her professional world postpartum. It wasn't that she felt any less competent. She knew she would continue to work hard and aim for excellence in the legal world. It was getting what she needed as a new, working mom that had her troubled.

I thought I was in some upside-down universe. I missed my daughter, but I loved being freer. That made me feel guilty. I was more tired than I had ever been. Finding a dedicated pumping space and then finding the time to pump felt like some kind of major accomplishment. I felt unsupported. It took me a while to figure out how to do both—how to be a mom and how to be back on the job.

When you spend all day in postpartum zone, going back to work can feel monumental. You've been immersed in baby world—its own unique, special, and sometimes grueling transition—and now it's time to jolt yourself back to "real life." The only problem is, the world you left before you had a baby will be different for you now that you're a new mom—not worse or better, just different—with its own set of challenges and, at times, very emotional changes.

I'll be honest: for me, I didn't cry at all the day I went back to work after I had my first baby. I thought I would. We were bonded, and I was fully prepared to sit under my desk with a box of tissues for the first few hours back in the office, but the feeling I had that first day was not one of sadness; it was one of pure relief. Though my colicky baby had turned a corner and I was finally getting more sleep, it was still hard to be at home. When I reentered the workplace, I found I was, in some ways, back to the old me. I could eat lunch with both hands. I had adult conversations with different people all day. Eventually, by the end of the day, I went back home to the child who I loved the most, more than anything else in the *whole* world. It was, by all measures in my book, totally ideal. If that's you too, you're in good company.

What if that's not you? Did you return to work already with a heavy mix of tears and regret? Take heart, and breath. You're also in good company. My return-to-work depression days hit after I had my second daughter and realized my last maternity leave with my last baby *ever* had come to an end. Her infancy was gentler, and I had a better support system during my maternity leave experience with her. If this is you, please believe me: It does get better. If you're somewhere in-between, that's OK too. Going back to work, for all moms, brings up a lot of emotions, some of which are conflicting and confusing. Remember, on the day you leave your infant son or infant daughter for the workplace, you are not abandoning your baby, and you *and* your baby will be OK. Most importantly, you can never be replaced. You will always be mom.

✂❀✂❀✂

Whatever your return to work mindset, consider these ways to make the transition easier.

Look at the Big Picture

At some point after you start working again, you're going to start doing a bunch of financial calculations when it comes to paying for child care. Maybe you are a new mom or maybe you are having your second child. You may realize that, by working, you're barely covering your child care costs, and the whole thing may feel like a giant waste. And, maybe for just a second or maybe for months, you may feel like you want to quit. Now, to each their own on the stay-at-home mom versus working mom front (I mean really, I think it's safe to say there's no need for working mom versus stay-at-home mom battles in this day and age, given how many of us work more or less at any given stage of motherhood, anyway). But, as *Candy Crush* creator Hope Cochran told me, "So many women who have babies in their late 20s and 30s do the (financial) equation on child care versus working and decide that it's not worth it to work. The equation is not about just those years. If you're choosing to not work because the financial equation doesn't make sense to you, you could be looking at the equation all wrong."

Consider Easing Back Into Work

Strongly consider requesting an ease-in schedule as you return to the workforce. Working several hours at a time or even half days can make the child care transition go more smoothly and can help you get over the stark contrast between staying home in baby land versus spending time at the office.

If you don't work independently, stay in touch with your manager or human resources representative throughout your maternity leave so you can have those conversations as your return to work date gets closer. Think about what would work best for your schedule, and ask for it. You'll never get what you don't ask for, and the worst your employer can say is no. Consider asking for a reduced schedule for the first month back (easing up to full time, for example, by working a few days per week at first), or, at minimum, start on a Thursday so the first week is short. Several top tech companies actually structure the first month back automatically as 2 days, 3 days, 4 days, and then finally a full week. If your employer accommodates telecommuting options or other alternative ways to clock hours for a few weeks, consider giving yourself and your postpartum state some grace by taking advantage of that flexibility.

If possible, go back at 80% time for the first month or 2. If you have paid time off (PTO) saved up, schedule a day or 2 off in the first month just to have a time on the calendar to catch up. If you don't have PTO to use for the ease-in schedule, you could also ask to use some of your leave time intermittently to create an ease-in plan.

Plan Ahead for Feeding Your Baby: Breastfeeding and Pumping

Know Your Rights

It wasn't that long ago that women had virtually no breastfeeding rights in the workplace, and, believe me, I've heard some horror stories about women cramped into tiny bathrooms while pumping even recently. The law, though, is on our side when it comes to pumping and work. Current federal regulations require employers to provide nursing employees with a private place to express milk throughout the day. The law states the amount of time should be "reasonable." Every lactating mom is different, but remember, you'll want to factor in enough time during each session to set up your pumping gear, pump, and then clean everything back up again.

Learn to Pump on the Go

I've pumped just about everywhere you can imagine—in the bathroom stall at a baseball game, at my desk, in the car...*everywhere*—because, when I first started breastfeeding, I decided that I would not be deterred by technical difficulties or by a lack of convenience. I wanted to be able to pump on trips, at the airport, at hotels, *and I did.* There are a lot of things I look back on in my first year of parenting that I could have done differently or wished I'd known more about, but this? This one I feel I knocked out of the park. Not because I'm so amazing but it was important to me and because I was intentional about it, and I was proud about the choices I made. Here's what you can do to make pumping successful.

Go Back to Lactation

Even if you feel like you have the "breastfeeding from your breast" thing down, pumping and feeding successfully is a whole other ball of wax. When you're home all day with your baby during maternity leave, your milk supply is often at its best. Once you go to work and are pumping consistently, that decreased stimulation to your nipples can sometimes affect your milk production. If that happens to you, meeting with a certified lactation specialist can help guide you as you make the transition to more pumping throughout the day.

Yes, social media groups can seem helpful when you start pumping, giving you tips and tricks and support that don't come in the pump manual, but remember that the members' advice is usually based only on their personal experiences. If you have questions or need support think about returning to a certified lactation specialist to guide you on this next part of your breastfeeding journey. Probably most importantly, the lactation specialist can measure you for the correct-sized pump if you haven't done this already—a critical step for making sure you don't injure your breasts or nipples in the pumping process and that your pumping sessions are efficient. Set up your appointment for about 1 month before you go back to your job, if possible.

Get a Good Pump

If you're planning on pumping a lot, you're going to want to invest in good equipment. It is important for the breast pump to be a double-electric pump, which means you can pump both breasts at the same time. It has an electric motor, preferably with an adjustment for different suction levels.

It also needs to work with a breast pump system, which means it's compatible with bottles for feeding, bottles for storing milk, cleaning supplies, cooler bags, freezer bags, and so on. You want all of this to work seamlessly together so you don't waste your precious time rigging a ton of parts together.

One hidden consideration? Your pump needs to have easy-to-find replacement parts. Most of the major brands out there should qualify. If your pump parts are not online or readily accessible at the store, you'll be frantic when you really need a pump accessory and you can't find one.

Most importantly—and this is not emphasized enough—you need something that is going to be *portable*. When I had my first daughter, I had this huge pump that needed to be plugged into a wall at all times to work. I quickly switched over to one that had extreme portability. (Note: For some moms with production issues, the pump efficiency is the most important factor, making other considerations seem frivolous. Follow the advice of your pediatrician and your lactation specialist.) Whichever setup you choose, most important is that you set it up and have it all sterilized *before* you have your baby. This is an awesome task to assign to a partner, but you'll be using it, so make sure you have a working knowledge of the pump yourself.

Buy Extra Parts

If your budget allows, have a spare set of pump parts at work, a set in your pump bag, and a set at home. You will forget something important one day and be so happy for the spare. In the same vein, carry a manual pump to use in case of emergency. Even more critical, if you have a pump that has to be plugged in, buy a compatible, rechargeable battery pack. Believe me, in the case of a power outage or a lack of power outlets, you will be happy you followed my advice. On the other hand, if you plan at all on traveling with your pump to conferences or for a getaway weekend, it pays to invest in a portable pump that doesn't require plugging in at all.

Do a Trial Run

Before you ever go back to work, do a half-day pumping trial. Have a child care provider (or a family member) stay with your baby for half the day while you learn how to pump and store your milk. Whatever your setup will be at the office, try to mimic the environment as much as possible. If you've arranged for a gradual return to work, this is an ideal way to get your feet wet as you start out. If you're starting at full speed, it's even more important to try out your pumping gear ahead of time.

Start Early to Avoid Bottle Refusal
Slow flow, fast flow, vented, preemie—the possibilities seem endless as you stand in the baby aisle and stare at the shelves. When moms-to-be are pregnant, trying to pick out the right bottles, and planning for their return to work postpartum, can be overwhelming. There's a lot of information out there on bottle-feeding but hardly any forewarnings about how to help babies take a bottle once they're already established exclusive breastfeeders. The lactation specialists I work with frequently see moms heading back to work who never bottle-fed at all during maternity leave, or who tried it a few times early on, called it good, but then struggled once they started back on the job.

To avoid bottle refusal, try bottle-feeding early and often, as soon as 1 month old (once latch and feeding patterns are well established). Not only does it help your baby get used to drinking apart from you, it also gives your partner a chance to bond with the baby too. This is a special and unique opportunity for them to experience.

When you do use the bottle, try 1 of 2 ways. First, try mimicking breastfeeding, holding your baby cradled in your arms like she's nursing—maybe even starting with the breast in her mouth then swiftly swapping your nipple out for a bottle (hopefully) before she notices. If your baby is on to you, looking up with a quizzical look and spitting out the silicone nipple, try for the opposite: hold her facing outward, maybe looking up at a fan or outside at the birds in the sky, and sneak the bottle to her lips while she's distracted. In this approach, you're trying to make bottle-feeding completely different from breastfeeding.

Don't be thrown off by a little resistance. Being at the breast is different from being at the bottle—one is warm and snuggly and the other...is a bottle. The rhythmic letdown is different, and the feel in the mouth is different. Some babies just will not do it at first. If your baby fights the bottle, take a second to breathe before becoming flustered. Most babies who refuse the bottle in the first few days after mom goes back to work get the hang of it relatively quickly (even if it feels like forever to their mothers).

Make Sure You're Up to Speed on Storage Guidelines
You worked hard for all that milk! Make sure it stays fresh and safe for your baby by following these guidelines when you're pumping.

Human Milk Storage Guidelines			
	Storage Location and Temperatures		
Type of Breast Milk	**Countertop 77°F (25°C) or colder** (room temperature)	**Refrigerator 40°F (4°C)**	**Freezer 0°F (−18°C) or colder**
Freshly Expressed or Pumped	Up to **4 hours**	Up to **4 days**	Within **6 months** is best. Up to **12 months** is acceptable.
Thawed, Previously Frozen	1–2 hours	Up to **1 day** (24 hours)	NEVER refreeze human milk after it has been thawed.
Leftover from a feeding (Baby did not finish the bottle.)		Use within **2 hours** after the baby is finished feeding.	

Reproduced from Division of Nutrition, Physical Activity, and Obesity, National Center for Chronic Disease Prevention and Health Promotion. Proper storage and preparation of breast milk. Centers for Disease Control and Prevention. Reviewed January 22, 2020. Accessed November 12, 2020. https://www.cdc.gov/breastfeeding/recommendations/handling_breastmilk.htm.

When Breastfeeding Doesn't Work Out: Formula Preparation and Storage

Like every good pediatrician out there, I could name the multiple benefits of breast milk and breastfeeding in my sleep. The fact is, though, breastfeeding failure rates are exceptionally high in the United States, and the working moms I know don't need to be guilted over and over about what works for them and for their children. I'm always trying to help moms reach their breastfeeding goals, but the reality is that it doesn't always go as planned or hoped. If breastfeeding just doesn't work for you, please remember this: *being a breastfeeder or a non-breastfeeder does not define you as a mom.* It's one small part of your motherhood journey. Being a mom is about so much more than breastfeeding.

If you're using formula, remember these storage and preparation tips.

Pay Attention to Formula Preparation

If you are formula feeding, take advantage of your ability to prepare ahead and to carry food portably. You can make a batch of formula in advance for the day (refrigerated continuously for up to 24 hours). Consider using a formula mixing pitcher for mixing larger amounts. This cuts down on the air bubbles that get introduced with shaking a bottle. Premeasured packets can help you feed your baby safely and easily if you're on the go (*The New Baby Blueprint: Caring for You and Your Little One.* 2020:106–107).

Be Safe When Storing Prepared Formula and When Heating Bottles

Once you prepare a bottle of formula, feed it to your baby or put it into the refrigerator within 1 hour. If it's been at room temperature for more than an hour, throw it out. If you make a bottle of formula for your baby and she doesn't drink the whole thing, discard it. You can prepare formula up to

24 hours ahead of time by storing it in the refrigerator (so that it doesn't form bacteria). If you open ready-made formula containers, they can be stored safely in the refrigerator for up to 48 hours (*The New Baby Blueprint: Caring for You and Your Little One*. 2020:107).

Take Caution When Heating Bottles

Just because most people heat their babies' bottles, it's not necessary. A lot of babies will tolerate cold or room temperature bottles of formula just fine, saving you headaches and time in the long run. If your baby prefers a warm bottle, never use a microwave to heat it. The microwave can create "hot spots" within the formula, leading to potential burns. Instead, run the bottle under hot or warm water for a few minutes, or use a pan of hot water to heat the liquid. Bottle warmers also work well. However you heat your baby's bottles, make sure to shake them well after heating and to test the formula temperature by placing a few drops onto the inside of your wrist to assure it's lukewarm (not hot) (*The New Baby Blueprint: Caring for You and Your Little One*. 2020:107).

Bonding With Your Baby

The internet can be a scary place, full of misinformation and also full of admonishments for new moms: Feed this, not that. Start showing your infant black-and-white flash cards immediately after they exit the womb to encourage brain development. Buy this. Watch out for *all of that*. It's dizzying, and it makes all kinds of new parents anxious with indecision over what activities to do with their new babies.

What really matters? Bonding. Downtime. Soft cuddles and lingering gazes into your baby's eyes. From the very beginning, your child builds attachment—the understanding that he's safe, secure, and protected—as you do very simple activities like talking and singing to him and as you learn to understand and read your baby's wants and needs.

Pediatricians see it every day in the newborn nursery. A new dad will talk softly to his fresh day-old baby girl, cradling her in his arms and whispering "I love you," and she will turn her tiny face toward him, almost cocking her head in his direction to make sure she hears every single sweet nothing. It's magical and it's incredibly simple. It doesn't require gadgets. It doesn't require developmental toys and tricks. It just requires 2 humans paying attention to only each other for a brief moment.

Babies grow into toddlers and toddlers to teens, but that need for human connection never, ever goes away. Technology and gadgets can't take its place. In fact, personal devices and screens are part of what's degrading our inter-actions and keeping us from building bonds with our peers, much less our children. We could save ourselves a whole lot of time and money if we committed to simplifying our kids' early interactions with us. So your baby never learns sign language and never gets a PhD in quantum physics in her first year after birth? She'll be OK. I promise. Your baby needs you, not fancy gadgets or gear.

It's going to get pretty boring after about 10 minutes of your mommy–baby gazing, so what then? When considering your own mental health, pick activities for bonding that also

● Connect you with other like-minded moms or mom groups that suit you.
● Get your mind and your body active with exercise.
● Get you outside in the fresh air whenever possible.

When considering child development, choose classes that facilitate play between you and your baby. Music immersion, mommy–baby exercise groups, and library time top my list.

The Night Before You Return and the First Week Back

The night before you go back to work for the first time, get organized. Make bottles for child care, make your lunch, lay your clothes out—whatever you need to make the morning run as smooth as possible. If you don't quite fit into all your old work clothes yet, try a clothing rental company to tide you over while you're still in a transitional body. These things take time, my friend. Dedicate a little time that evening with your partner to review your week and talk about any special logistics you have to manage. Being a working parent is 150% about logistics, so the more you have those worked out from the get-go, the more you can concentrate on your emotional transition to this next stage of life.

It can be tempting to overplan your weekends when you head back to the office because you miss your family time (or your alone time) so much. For your sanity, though, think about doing the opposite for the first few months. Don't pack your first few weekends full of outings and activities. Instead, plan to nap and adjust to a new level of complication and fatigue (which gets better, by the way).

Back-to-Work Checklist

✓ Pump parts sterilized and organized

✓ Milk thawed or formula prepared

✓ Groceries purchased for the week

✓ Extra nursing pads, pump cleaning equipment packed

✓ Child care provider informed on your child's sleep, feeding, and care routines

✓ Work schedule posted in a visible place for child care provider and partner

✓ House organized and tidy

✓ Lunch, healthy snacks, and water bottle packed

✓ Clothing ironed or pressed

(continued)

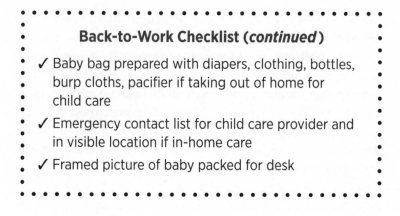

Back-to-Work Checklist (*continued*)

✓ Baby bag prepared with diapers, clothing, bottles, burp cloths, pacifier if taking out of home for child care

✓ Emergency contact list for child care provider and in visible location if in-home care

✓ Framed picture of baby packed for desk

ↄↄↄↄↄ

Going back to work with a new baby can be incredibly daunting. I wanted to write something here about how it's also incredibly amazing, but I'm committed to being honest with you. It can be tough. It can be exhausting. It's full of steep learning curves. Yes, yes, it's also totally liberating to pee by yourself and to eat without interruption, but, for most moms, it's bittersweet. Take it slow. Focus on using your time when you are home to bond, not on your to-do list. Develop a sustainable feeding plan. Invest in quality care. Above all, remember, do what's right for you and your family, not what's right for the rest of the world.

Chapter 7

Choosing Child Care Options

When we treat children's play as seriously as it deserves, we are helping them feel the joy that's to be found in the creative spirit. It's the things we play with and the people who help us play that make a great difference in our lives.

—Fred Rogers

Choosing a child care option can be an overwhelming process. You want to find the perfect option for your child and your family. I understand. I did too. The people who will care for your child will strongly influence the way your kids grow up and see the world around them. And for that reason, choosing a child care option is one of the most important decisions you will make for your family.

Deciding on a child care option that works best for you and your family is highly personal and depends, ultimately, on your individual needs and situation. Is one type of care better than another? If you look to clickbait articles like, "Are Children in Daycare More Aggressive Than Their Peers?" or "Do Kids Raised by Nannies Really Turn Out OK?" you'll likely be confused.

Where's the truth? It lies somewhere in the middle. Our best evidence for the effect of child care on social, emotional,

Portions of this chapter are adapted from Casares W. Finding a child care provider. In: *The New Baby Blueprint: Caring for You and Your Little One*. American Academy of Pediatrics; 2020:63–75.

and intellectual development comes from a longitudinal study by the Eunice Kennedy Shriver National Institute of Child Health and Human Development. The study followed kids from a diverse background in a variety of care settings for 15 years starting in 1991. The study found that, not surprisingly, the kind of care a child receives—nanny care, child care, preschool, parent, or other—is not the most important. What matters most? The child's environment when *not* in care. Children raised in warm, responsive, appropriately stimulating home settings did best, no matter where they spent their days.

There were some nuanced findings that deserve mention. When children were in child care center or preschool center settings, the quality of those center programs mattered immensely. High-quality settings, including those with a high ratio of well-trained adults to children, were associated with better social, language, and cognitive developmental outcomes.

The amount of time spent in nonparental care influenced outcomes too, as did the child's age when he or she first entered care, though not to the same degree. Kids who spent more than 30 hours a week in nonparental care settings had statistically higher levels of behavioral problems, including aggression and lack of cooperation, than did their counterparts who had fewer hours in these settings. Children younger than 3 years were less likely to experience stress when they were cared for at home, whereas those at high-quality preschools with well-trained staff after the age of 3 had the best outcomes. Again, though, a warm, supportive family environment was an overriding factor, and a high-quality child care setting with loving, invested staff outside the home was better than a bored or stressed parent or an uninventive nanny at home.

As you decide on what form of child care best fits your family's needs, you'll find positive and negative scenarios for each. There just isn't a best kind of child care. Your decision will be based on a number of benefits and drawbacks, budgets and must-haves, and, in the end, priorities and what feels best. Here are some strategies for deciding which kind of care aligns best with your needs and deciding on a specific provider or care center.

Child Care Centers

When you begin the process of finding a child care center for your child, it's a great idea to talk with other parents in your area and do your homework with your local child care resource and referral agency (CCR&R). They compare child care centers based on the same objective criteria called Quality Rating and Improvement Systems. You can find your local CCR&R at https://www.childcareaware.org. Find recommendations from other parents in your neighborhood who also have children and are in your same situation. Depending on where you live, child care centers may have a waiting list. Do a little research while you're pregnant to make sure you reserve a spot on a place that you are interested in. Here are some important things to look for in a child care center.

● Look for child care centers that share your goals for your kids as they grow. You want a provider that is going to teach your children important messages about forming healthy relationships and contributing to society and that help build resilience.

● Centers that share these goals are especially attuned to these areas of focus: they have a strong understanding of general child development but pay attention to each child's individual needs.

● They provide a safe and clean environment where the children they serve can learn in age-appropriate ways.

● They focus on language and building communication and social skills on the basis of positive behavior management.

● They work alongside parents as a team.

Child care centers can provide amazing benefits for many families. First and foremost, high-quality centers are physically designed specifically for kids, and the curriculum they follow is also specifically designed to promote learning. The benefit of a child care center is that it is not dependent on 1 caregiver's availability day to day. Even if 1 teacher is sick or takes an unexpected leave, your child will still have dependable care. Child care centers are also a place where children and their parents can develop strong communities, and you will find they can be a source of friendship not just for the kids who attend but also for their parents. The caregivers can learn from each other and from ongoing education efforts.

The best centers are social, boisterous places where children enjoy varied, joyful, stimulating activities with their peers. Employer-based on-site child care centers can be especially convenient for drop-off and pickup and also for lunchtime nursing sessions or quick drop-ins to cuddle a little one.

Working mom Mariana beamed at her son's 6-month appointment. "I love being able to run over for a lunchtime breastfeeding session. Since my work has a child care next to my office, I feel like I have the best of all worlds. I can check up on Sam whenever I want to; we 'go to work' together; and he's just a hop, skip, and jump away from me at all times."

Some aspects of child care centers can be stressful for families. The vibe of a classroom is dependent on a well-trained teacher managing many children for hours. If a teacher's skills aren't up to par and the classroom can be chaotic, that can be stressful for sensitive children or for those who are particularly sensitive. Centers generally require specific hours for drop-off and pickup. For many parents, getting up and out the door in the morning with infants and toddlers in tow can feel stressful and rushed. Centers generally assign your child based on their age to a classroom, which gives parents less choice when it comes to the specific person who will spend the most time with their child.

One major source of stress to any father or mother thinking about child care is the increased risk of illness. A child in child care will be exposed to more germs daily than a child in a one-on-one or nanny share setting just because of the sheer number of other children she's around. Yes, over time that can contribute to a stronger immune system, but, for some families, it can mean a world of hurt every winter. Every child is different—some kids seem to skate by without a cold or rash—but unfortunately for others it can be a recurring theme.

"For the first year of Aiden's life, I thought maybe there was something wrong with him," said working mom Josie. "He had constant colds. He was home more than at child care. I started thinking his immune system was weaker than everybody else's."

Even though a nanny or smaller in-home setting can seem more expensive on the surface, you should factor in all the scenarios. Consider your cost-benefit child care analysis for potential sick days if your child is in a group setting. As a working mother, especially in my profession, it's not impossible to take a day off, but it is a huge inconvenience to my patients and to my business partners. I look for ways to avoid my kids catching major illnesses in the first place, so that I don't have to miss work.

Not all the statistics on child care center–related illness are negative, though. One study, published in *Pediatrics* by researchers from the Netherlands in 2016, showed that being in child care as an infant increased the risk that a child developed acute gastroenteritis (aka a stomach bug) in the first year after birth but also found child care was a protective factor until at least age 6. In fact, the kids who went to child care before 1 year of age had more gastroenteritis earlier on but fewer illnesses than their non–child care counterparts as they got older. Rates of gastroenteritis seemed to even out by age 6, which is as far as the study went. A 2014 study by the same scientists found a similar trend in upper respiratory infections and ear infections: kids who went to child care in their first year after birth had more ear infections and upper respiratory infections in the early years but fewer later on.

"Once Aiden got through that first year, it was like he developed a coat of armor," working mom Josie said. "In the end, I wasn't happy about missing work in those first 12 months, but I found it wasn't nearly as big a deal as he got older. Plus, I learned a lot about common colds during that time. Now I feel like I'm a pro. I'm not nearly so scared when he does (rarely) get sick."

Look for these markers of a high-quality child care center.

High Caregiver to Child Ratio

Make sure the staffing ratios at the center fall in line with national standards. Lower staffing ratios mean a caregiver has more time to spend with each individual child, including yours. It means more time for snuggles, hugs, reading—all the things that build connection and secure attachment for a little one to his or her "people."

A Vision-Driven Owner or Company

What are the center's policies about things like discipline, cleanliness, medication administration, and disaster preparedness? Are there background checks on all employees? What are the rules about exclusion for minor illness? If your child care center has many locations and is part of a larger system, make sure you're familiar with the company's vision for care. What educational philosophy do they ascribe to? What are their goals for the children and families in their fold? How do they treat their teachers? Do they provide health insurance for their employees? Do they require flu vaccination for their employees? Is there a provider smoking policy? Is there a set program for education and improvement/ongoing education and redirection for wayward caregivers? What policies are in place to ensure children are kept safe at drop-off and pickup and while in the center's care? Your state's Quality Rating and Improvement System is your go-to source for information about child care centers in your local area.

An Invested Director and Teacher

If there are multiple sites for the child care center, meet or connect electronically with the director for the site your child may attend. Ask how long the director has been with the organization and about his or her management style. You want to know how involved the director is with the classrooms and what the relationship is like with teachers. Likewise, find out how available the director is to parents when they have questions. Is it easy to catch her at pickup? Does she make herself available at drop-off or at parent education nights? How does she communicate the children's activities with moms and dads?

Similarly, research the center's teachers. What education or qualifications do they have? Most child care websites include teacher biographies where you can find out about their training and ongoing education, background, and, often, how long they've been working there. If most teachers have been with the center for less than 6 months, take pause.

A Welcoming, Safe Atmosphere

Take a tour to really get a true sense of how the center runs and how staff interact with the children they care for. Above all, watch for how well the teachers pay attention and speak to their students and how

(continued)

genuinely interested they are in them. What do they do when kids have behaviors that need redirection or when they misbehave? Are they on the students' level, speaking in a way that seems nurturing and kind? Do they talk more with each other or with the kids? Do they respond quickly and appropriately? Does the environment look clean and well organized? Are children actually playing with the equipment set out for them? Do the children and staff seem happy? For more information on this topic, go to https://www.childcareaware.org.

The "Choosing a Child Care Center" table is a good guide to follow when it comes to choosing a child care center and staff to child ratio sizes.

Choosing a Child Care Center		
Age	Maximum Child–Staff Ratio*	Maximum Group Size*
12 months	3:1	6
13–35 months	4:1	8
3-year-olds	7:1	14
4-year-olds	8:1	16
5-year-olds	8:1	16
6- to 8-year-olds	10:1	20
9- to 12-years-olds	12:1	24

*As recommended by the American Academy of Pediatrics.

Reproduced from American Academy of Pediatrics. Choosing a child care center. HealthyChildren.org. Updated November 21, 2015. Accessed November 12, 2020. https://www.healthychildren.org/English/family-life/work-play/Pages/Choosing-a-Childcare-Center.aspx

Parents should pay attention to these special considerations for children of different ages.

Babies

- Do teachers appear warm and loving?
- Does the environment allow for exploration and play?
- Do teachers seem responsive to crying and diapering needs?
- What are the breastfeeding policies at the facilities?
- Can teachers see babies at all times, even when they're sleeping?
- Does the center follow the American Academy of Pediatrics Back to Sleep policies?
- Do teachers hold babies for cuddling and for feeding?
- Are all babies on the exact same schedule, or is there flexibility for individual needs?
- Can parents visit whenever they want to, and are they encouraged to do so?
- Are diaper changing and feeding locations separated?

Toddlers

- Are the lots of options for activities?
- Is the room arranged so children can play in small groups and one-on-one?
- Do mealtimes act as an opportunity to socialize and develop basic skills, like drinking from a cup or using utensils?
- Is reading an emphasized activity?
- Does the schedule allow for some flexibility based on individual student needs?
- Is screen time limited?
- Is outdoor play encouraged?
- Are diaper changing and feeding locations separated?

(continued)

- Are there plenty of sinks for handwashing for children and caregivers?
- Do the caregivers speak often to the children and ask them questions?

Preschool

- Is the room arranged in learning centers, including music, art, science, and reading?
- Does the teacher post a calendar with structured activities planned throughout the day?
- Do activities appear to vary day by day?
- Is social play emphasized through activities and play stations?
- Are there play structures and opportunities for outside play?
- Are children active or mostly sedentary?

Working mom Karen told me, "I could tell from the moment I walked in that Mirielle's child care was the right choice. There was art everywhere. The teachers all greeted her with smiling faces. On the tour, I heard singing and laughing. I just knew it in my gut it was the best place for her."

Use the "Child Care Center Sample Questionnaire" to help keep you organized as you visit and view different child care centers in preparation for your baby's arrival.

Nanny Care

Nannies provide individualized care in a home setting, allowing flexibility for those with inconsistent or nontraditional work schedules and when kids get sick. Without the hustle of dressing, feeding, and transporting kids to a center or another person's home, having a nanny can reduce stress for parents throughout the week. Nannies can provide a wide array of

Child Care Center Sample Questionnaire

Certifications
• Is the center licensed and accredited by the state?
• What level of education and what certifications does staff have?
• What ongoing trainings do you complete with staff about child development and behavioral management?

Finances
• What are the daily or monthly tuition rates?
• What's the financial policy for late pickup?
• How much does it cost to secure a spot on the waiting list?

Schedules
• What are the daily drop-off and pickup windows?
• What is the daily schedule, including naps?
• Are there preplanned holiday or vacation week closures throughout the year?

Behavior and Child Development
• What is your center's educational philosophy or care philosophy?
• How do you handle conflicts between children?
• How much time is spent outside? Is there a dedicated outdoor play area at the facility?
• Do you provide daily reports for kids' behaviors or activities?
• What are the expectations around potty training and diaper changes?

Staffing
• What is the staff turnover rate?
• How do you screen employees for hire?
• How many children are in each room and at the facility in total?
• What is the staff to child ratio at the facility?
• When do kids typically move up from an infant room to a toddler room or from a toddler room to a preschool room?

Feeding
• How do you handle frozen or pumped breast milk preparation or formula preparation?
• What is served for meals or snacks? Do parents need to provide food?

Safety and Health
• What is the sick policy for children and for staff?
• How often and how do you sanitize the toys and materials at the center?
• What are the vaccination rates among children currently in the center?
• How do you keep your facility safe and secure?
• Do you ever transport children outside the facility? If so, how?

(continued)

Child Care Center Sample Questionnaire (*continued*)

Parent Involvement
• Do you provide parent-child development education opportunities?
• What is the policy on parents visiting the child care center during the day?

opportunities and experiences for the children they care for that are specifically tailored to the temperaments and interests of those kids. The best nannies care deeply about making one-on-one connections with "their kids" and exposing them to myriad diverse, play-based opportunities.

Working mom Laurel said, "I don't think I could do my job without a nanny. I can't get to a child care pickup by 6:00 pm. I don't want to have to worry about being late if I have an afternoon meeting that runs over."

The downside? Nannies can be expensive, especially when you have only 1 child (once you have a second child who also needs care while you work, child care and nanny costs can be less discrepant). If a nanny's not inventive or doesn't have a lot of motivation, kids may not do much learning or exploring at all. Kids with nannies can be more socially isolated unless the caregiver actively seeks out opportunities for playdates and classes, which can cost even more. If a nanny quits unexpectedly or is sick herself, scrambling for backup care can be daunting, especially if children are tightly bonded with only them. Likewise, if a nanny doesn't meet your expectations or doesn't fit your needs over time, it can be tough to make a clean break without affecting your kids emotionally.

Working mom Michelle said, "I felt like I was letting a family member go. Deciding to move to child care after 3 years with our nanny was one of the toughest decisions I've had to make as a new mom. She'd become like a sister to me. Sure, we kept some type of relationship with her once we moved on, but I didn't think it would be so hard. We both cried."

Finding a great nanny can be more nuanced than finding a child care center given the personal nature of hiring one. Unless they're listed with a professional nanny company, few have personal websites or even résumés that speak fully to their wealth of experience and caregiving style. Don't be lulled into thinking hiring through a professional nanny company is the only way to find reliable, qualified candidates, though. Friends, family, coworkers, and local social media mom groups are often great sources for initial nanny referrals, but be sure all candidates have thorough background checks, verified CPR and first aid training, health insurance, and ongoing training.

On caregiver search sites specifically designed for finding care, they'll make it easy for you to narrow down your top contenders —they'll allow you to create a profile and a job posting where you then filter through applicants and set up in-person interviews. From there, you can sign up for a paid trial during which the caregiver cares for your child for just an hour or so while you're still in the house so that you can make sure you feel comfortable. Here's the secret, though: it's not about where; it's about how. It doesn't matter what site you use or what friend makes an initial suggestion. It matters what process you go through to attract, evaluate, and ultimately decide on your final hire.

Here Are My Top 4 Strategies for Finding an Amazing Caregiver

Focus on the Details

Be thorough and specific as you outline your needs. Make sure you've covered all the things that really matter to you as you create your job description so that the standard of applicant is raised from the get-go and you don't attract people who aren't a good fit. This is my exact job post when I was looking:

My husband and I are currently pregnant with our first baby and are due with our little girl mid-October. I will have about three months off work and then will go back. We are looking for a great nanny to care for our little one at our home on the days I work. We need someone sporadically starting in October and consistently starting in January. In mid-October to mid-January, it would be for babysitting, to get to know us and her, so I can get a break some days and so I could fill in at my work some days if needed before I officially go back.

We could work out what would work for your schedule, but we don't have specific guaranteed hours in mind. Starting mid-January, it would be part time guaranteed two days per week (the days I am working, which are Tuesday and Friday) plus whatever works for both parties for extra babysitting/extra days, etc. We're looking for someone who could for sure commit to working with us until our daughter is one but possibly for longer, depending on our needs plus your needs.

Stay Serious

Present yourself in a way that attracts the person you want working for you. Get a contract together so that you look professional. Delineate vacation and sick day expectations, salary, work hours, and household duties. Online child care search sites such as Care.com (www.care.com) and Sittercity (www.sittercity.com) will often have free downloadable templates you can use as a jumping-off point. Refine your contract according to your individual needs.

Plan Ahead

My nanny told me that when she saw my job posting, she was really impressed, because I posted it about 3 months before I had my baby. I didn't need regular care for 6 months from the time of the job posting. She said she loved that. However, if you are about to have your baby and you are just now trying to find care, please try to stay calm. All is not lost.

She explained to me, "If you are a really serious nanny and you're looking for a transition, you don't just try to find a position 2 weeks ahead of time. You look 4 to 6 months ahead."

Similarly, if you are searching for child care centers, expect high-demand sites to have long waiting lists. Start your search early if possible.

Be Choosy

Feel free to weed out those who don't quite measure up. This is your kid we're talking about. You want a caregiver you feel great about. Filter out applicants who don't present themselves professionally (by having spelling or grammatical errors), who don't have the quality of experience you're looking for, or who don't fit your style. If you start your search early, you're more likely to allow enough time to find a good pool of applicants from which to choose.

Sometimes when you meet someone in person, it becomes even clearer that the person is right (or wrong) for you. Use your gut to make your final decision. Check multiple references. When someone said, "I know this is a big deal and I can tell you without reservation that you will be so happy you chose her—she's like family at this point," I knew I had found a winner.

Stay Real

It's important to know the things you really want from a caregiver. Start to make a list of your checkbox items. To me, what was really important for example was that my caregiver was certified in CPR (cardiopulmonary resuscitation). That was a must. Here are the 5 characteristics that I found on the top of my list.

Intuitive

I wanted someone who was intuitive and confident. In my experience, this comes only from real experience. As a pediatrician, once you've seen a hundred ear infections, you can spot one a mile away. The same hard-earned confidence goes for caregivers.

If someone has "more than 10 years' experience" on her résumé but it means occasionally babysitting a neighbor, it doesn't count as much as someone who has cared for 4 families over the course of 5 to 10 years, with children ranging in ages from infancy to 15 years. People like that probably know their stuff.

Working mom Meredith told me, "Madison was the best nanny. You could just tell she was a pro. She showed up to the trial run for my kids with an art project. 'I figured I should try to win them over on day one,' was her explanation. I mean…."

Trustworthy

I wanted someone who was trustworthy. When we had our in-person interview with our nanny, I told her I was looking for someone who could call me for anything but who felt comfortable in most situations so that the person wouldn't need to unless there was a real emergency.

Turns out that was what our nanny was looking for too. She told me that one of the main reasons *she* chose *us* was because she knew she wouldn't be micromanaged all day long on things she knew a lot about. She presented herself as a professional and expected to be treated in the same way. She, of course, defers to my direction if needed, but because she is so trustworthy and confident, I hardly ever feel the need to redirect.

Loving

I wanted someone who would deeply love my kids. I think sometimes this can be one of the most daunting aspects of this whole search, but the reality is, when you are searching for someone to care for your children regularly, it matters that they are loved during that time (of course, in a way that keeps your kids safe and that has appropriate boundaries), not just "watched."

You can never be completely sure how people will care for your child, but you can tell a lot from the way they talk about prior children they've cared for. When you ask potential caregivers about their prior experience, listen carefully. My nanny spoke warmly about each of her past jobs. I could tell the children she took care of were like family to her as I heard her thoughtfully recount some of her best memories with them. The way she described her experiences gave a clue as to the way she felt about each of those relationships. Her references verified that family vibe, specifically mentioning how they included her in special celebrations and sometimes even family vacations.

Working mom Lisa said, "We took our nanny everywhere with us because she was an extension of our nuclear family. I learned so much from her early on that I realized I could be prideful about the fact *I* was the mom, or I could decide I was one lucky mama to have her around and just lean in to her expertise and presence. When I did that, life got easier."

As a mom, this takes a little bit of letting go. It means that your children will form a relationship with someone who is not you, that they might one day call your nanny "Mom" or "Dad" inadvertently, or that it may sometimes feel as if they love your nanny (*gulp!*) more than they love you. I feel your pain. Your children might very well come to love their caregiver, and that would be the *best-case* scenario, in the end. When I finally put aside my pride and didn't let that sabotage my nanny search efforts, I was more successful.

Knowledgeable

I wanted someone who had a solid understanding of child development. I knew that eventually, my nanny would be the one to discipline my kids during the day. At first, it would be all roses and sunshine while they were cute and cuddly, but if I was in this for the long haul (which I was), there would come a time she would be handling tantrums and time-outs. I wanted her to be comfortable with this and for it to be second nature to her.

Let me be clear: this doesn't mean a caregiver has to take official courses in child development. It also doesn't necessarily mean that a caregiver can quote experts in the field of behavioral management (can you?). It means that caregivers can walk you through what they would do if a tricky situation came up with your child, with the explanation making you say, "That is perfectly OK with me," or even, "Wow, I would never have thought to do that! That's a genius idea!"

Working mom Shelly told me in the clinic, "I can't believe how helpful it is to have another problem solver in my house. I love that I can brainstorm how to deal with my son's tantrums with the person who deals with them on a daily basis just like I do."

A Good Fit

I wanted someone I actually liked. This is so important. You really have to make sure that the person you hire is someone you would be OK spending time with or, even better, would want to spend time with. Caregivers don't need to be your best friend, but, odds are, you will develop a friendship with them as you share the responsibility of raising your kids together. If you are irritated by your caregiver half the time, the odds of this all working out will start to wear on you. Spend time in your interview asking a bit about your potential employee so that you have a good sense of the person you are inviting into your home.

If this child care option is something you would like to look into, create a list of questions you would ask a potential caregiver. Take a look at a sample nanny questionnaire to begin your search.

Nanny Sample Questionnaire

Experience
- Number of families you have nannied for and ages of children
- Length of time with other families
- Specific experience with newborns, especially using safe sleep techniques like back to sleep

Availability
- Current hours of availability
- Other commitments (eg, school, other families, part-time jobs)
- Upcoming vacation needs and anticipated time-off needs

Health
- Vaccination status
- Smoking and other substance use status

Certifications and Education
- CPR (cardiopulmonary resuscitation) and first aid certification status
- Child development knowledge and experience
- Comfort level with health issues (eg, fevers, colds, emergencies, special needs); knowledge about giving medications if needed
- Driver's license status; prior infractions

Favorite Ages and Activities With Kids
- Knowledge of local kid-friendly venues
- Favorite local parks, swimming pools, and classes

Handling Difficult Situations
- Describe a time a baby was crying uncontrollably and you had to figure out why.
- Describe a difficult situation you've had with a toddler and how you solved it.
- Describe an emergency you've had to deal with.

Negative or Positive Past Work Experiences
- Describe what went well or what was frustrating.
- Describe a "deal breaker" for you when finding a nanny position.

Additional Tasks
- Open to light housecleaning or cooking?
- Able to transport kids via car or public transportation?
- Knowledge of using car seats and booster seats depending on the age of the children

(continued)

> **Nanny Sample Questionnaire (*continued*)**
>
> **Other Families and Hobbies**
> • Open to playdates with other children?
> • Any special hobbies (eg, art, music, other languages you would incorporate into child care)?

Family Child Care

Sharing care with another family (or few families) you trust can be a smart way to reap the social benefits of a child care center while maintaining a homelike environment for your child. Official family child care must adhere to specific licensing standards similar to but not the same as larger child care centers do and should follow safety guidelines. However, because there are generally fewer children and 1 or 2 dedicated teachers, turnover is less of an issue, and your child's circle of contact with other children is smaller, which theoretically means less exposure to illness. In-home child care and nanny shares can also provide more flexibility throughout the day on the basis of individual children's needs and desires. Parents also enjoy widening their friendship base with other families who attend, and children who spend their days together in these settings often become fast friends.

Working mom Helen said, "I like that I'm not in a big care center but that she's not just one-on-one. Now we have friends we would have never had—friends that, hopefully, will last through her childhood (or at least until kindergarten)."

There are drawbacks to in-home centers just like for any other setting. If one child in the mix requires more attention or has special circumstances, an in-home care center may not have the resources or staff to address their needs while providing quality learning opportunities to other students. Limited staff also may mean that if 1 child or caregiver gets sick, you're back on duty and need to take time off work. The curriculum provided may not be as robust or varied as in a larger child care setting. Finally, if the caregiver's own child is part of the share or in the home, your child may not be fully prioritized in the case of illness or day-to-day attention.

If you're considering an in-home setup, make sure to tour every area where your child receives care to ensure cleanliness and safety. The diapering and food preparation locations should be distinct and separate. Ask tough questions like you would when considering a larger care center: How do children spend their days? What are the specific policies on illness, feeding, and parent involvement? Is there a backup provider in case of caregiver illness? How are parents informed about how a child fares throughout the day? If you're not satisfied, how much notice do you have to give to resign from care?

Make sure you meet all other families involved and are in alignment about expectations and goals. One working mom I met in clinic told me she didn't take this step and regretted it after a few months into the arrangement. "The other families in our family child care center didn't have the same needs ours did. Eventually, we had to move on, but if I'd known that ahead of time, it would have really influenced my decision-making."

Family and Friends

Sometimes a large network of friends and family can come in handy when you need someone to care for your kids, whether it's for a dinner date or a yoga class, so you can get some time for yourself. If you have a family member whom you really trust, that person would be a wonderful caregiver to your children. And sometimes that free care (or significantly reduced cost) can come in handy.

Working mom Maria said, "I loved having my mom as my daughter's primary caretaker. I've always felt close to my parents, and they really enjoyed spending extra time with their

THE WORKING MOM BLUEPRINT

granddaughter. Because they had the extra time and resources I didn't at that stage of the game, she enjoyed all kinds of experiences I would have never been able to offer her mid-week, if at all. Lunch at the park, playdates with friends—they did it all because they could and they wanted to. Sure, we had our moments, but on the whole it was a blessing."

The downside to this arrangement? Unfortunately, some-times these arrangements can get complicated because you are relying on them to do things the way you want. There is no formal employer–employee relationship. The family member's philosophy may be entirely different than your own (yes, even if that family member is a parent who raised you). Sometimes addressing concerns about daily schedules or approaches to your child's misbehavior with a friend or family member can be tricky, depending on your relationship with that person. Are you the type of person who will be able to handle someone's criticisms about your child's idio-syncrasies? Will it feel personal if someone questions your parenting style? Can you handle hearing about more screen time than you'd normally allow, missed naps for the sake of errands, or snacks that aren't on your preferred list?

Involving friends and family means setting specific expec-tations for your needs and your child's needs, keeping lines of communication open, and developing a pretty thick skin. It also means deciding when you'll let the chips fall where they may (as long as there are no major safety violations) if things aren't to your exact specifications and when you'll be most concerned about holding others to your standards on the issues you care most about (or being humble enough to realize your way wasn't best after all).

Paid caregivers will also vary in their willingness or ability to meet your expectations, but it's a little easier when deal-ing with an employee because you are *paying employees*. If it doesn't work out, you can usually end or alter your relation-ship with significantly less dramatic fallout. If the caregiving prowess or style doesn't quite measure up, you can choose to find someone new without the emotional considerations that come with personal relationship negotiations. On the flip side, it can be difficult for friends and family to understand or respect your boundaries or your parenting style. Sometimes you have to make a hard decision—is it worth it financially to muddy the friend and family waters, and, if it is, will you be able to let go of the smaller things that irk you?

Working mom Rema said, "My parents were just so old school. I didn't realize how rigid they would be with my twins, and, when I tried to talk to them about it, they said I could find another situation if I couldn't let them be in charge when they watched them. In the end, we made a switch."

The Most Important Caregiver Consideration

All child care choices are extremely personal. What might work for one family may not work for another. The best option may even vary from child to child within a family. From my experiences with families, my top picks are nannies, family members, and in-home child care settings for kids younger than 3 years. Once kids reach preschool age, the need for structure and social skill development outweighs the home care aspect. At that point, a mix of preschool and sitter/nanny is my top choice. Of course, budget often comes into play, and traditional child care settings with quality, reliable caregivers are a great option too.

I care most about quality care settings—options that provide a safe space where kids can build deep, one-on-one connections with their caregivers and peers and that is a place where kids do not get sick frequently (very important for all working parents). The program or person also needs to provide the level of flexibility you need. Finally, you want the adults caring for your child to have the same parenting goals and values you do, backed by a working knowledge of the core principles of successful caregiving. This could be in the care of a child care center, an in-home child care setting, a nanny, a nanny share, a friend, or a relative. The setting is less important than the atmosphere, structure, and people there.

Focus on finding experienced, quality providers. Like most things in life, what really matters when it comes to child care is that you feel comfortable and confident with your choice. The exact location or setup—child care center, nanny share, in-home child care, nanny care, or family care—matters less. Just make sure you find quality caregivers who share your goals and values, and consider each member of your caregiving team just that—an important part of your child's village, but not more important than what happens when your child is at home with you. Family environment trumps all. Finding care can be stressful, but it's also very exciting. You're building your village; you're hiring the person who will be there for your kids alongside you, nurturing, guiding, and caring for the person or people you love best. You'll find amazing people waiting in the wings to work with you.

While you contemplate the best option for you and your family, use the "Child Care Option Comparison Chart" to help make your decision.

Child Care Option Comparison Chart

Factor	Child Care Center	Nanny	Nanny Share	Family Member	Other
Cost					
Convenience					
Pickup/ Drop-off Flexibility					
Cognitive Stimulation					
Socialization Opportunities					
Sick Day Policy					
Holiday/ Vacation Closures					
Other					

Chapter 8

Taking Care of Toddlers and Elementary School Kids

Prioritizing and Supporting the People You Love Most

The most important thing in life is knowing the most important things in life.

—*David F. Jakielo*

*M*y daughter asks me almost every morning if it's a workday. "Mama, are you staying home today?" she asks, hopeful I'll be spending the morning snuggling with her instead of heading out the door. Usually I say, "No, today is a workday," but, every once in a while, I purposefully say yes, especially when it really counts.

It really counted a few months back, when she told me about a creative dance performance coming up at school. I caught her practicing in the front yard and writing dance steps on her arm in preparation one night. She was in my bedroom, staring in the mirror making surprised, then happy, then sad faces over and over again, trying to get all the emotional expression portions just right.

Actually, at first I had to tell her that I couldn't come. I explained to her that her grandma and sister would attend because I had a work meeting that I couldn't reschedule. It way too often feels like there are a million requests for attention from all angles—that there's never enough time in the day for everything.

"No, Mama," she said, looking me directly in the eye. "I need you there." Her little lip quivered. I stopped and looked right back at her, right in her eyes. There I saw an intense desire to be seen and heard—to be counted in my calculations about what's important and what's worth my time.

I was there for my daughter's magical moment on the stage. I decided to be there. I can't be there every time, but I chose specifically to be there when it really mattered to her. I moved my meeting and I rearranged my day. She looked me right in the eyes in that moment too, but this time, she was beaming, dancing, leaping across the floor of the school gym with an audience of peers and parents at 9:25 on a Friday morning.

As a working mother, I can't always make it to each performance or event, but moments like that make me take a second to pause and reflect on some bigger questions, like, "Why did I have kids?" No, seriously. When we have to juggle and rearrange and find ourselves flustered by fitting our kids into our lives, it's worth it to take a step back. What was it that made you decide to enter motherhood? Was it a box you wanted to check off your list? Did you figure, "It's now or never"? Or did you imagine your life richer, fuller, and more meaningful with a baby in your arms and a toddler on your hip—better because you had someone you knew you would love no matter what—that special kind of love that only parents know for their own little ones?

I bet I know the answer. It's the same for almost every mom I meet. Yet, somehow, along the way, it's hard to remember that having kids is something the vast majority of us choose to do in this day and age—that, even though it makes life more exhausting, it also is what makes life amazing.

Children, especially from birth to 5 years of age, need security and consistency to form self-esteem, develop resilience, and develop lasting healthy relationships with their caregivers. To do that, they need our time and attention. They need to know that in this rapid-fire, whirlwind world, they have a special place in our hierarchies that no one else can take. Prioritizing and supporting our kids means remembering they are among the people we love most. This goes for dads too, by the way, but since this is a book for working moms, let's stay focused.

Setting Aside Time to Connect Deeply With Our Children

Our kids may not need us to spend our every waking hour with them, but they do need us to spend a substantial amount of time with them. A few moments here and there are just not going to cut it. They don't deserve our leftovers. Kenneth R. Ginsburg, MD, MS Ed, FAAP, got real on this subject when he wrote in *Building Resilience in Children and Teens: Giving Kids Roots and Wings*

> In our overscheduled lives, we often talk of making *quality time* for our children. I agree—a few moments, when parents are truly present and undistracted, can be most meaningful. At the expense of saying something unpopular, though, *quantity* matters too. All parents are stretched to fulfill multiple obligations, but we need to make available as much time as possible for our children. To some extent, the quality of our time with them is influenced by the quantity of that time. I'm not suggesting that you quit your day job. I am saying that

there will be more opportunities to listen if we spend more time with our children. We won't always be there for the crises or heart-to-heart moments, but the more time we spend with them, the more likely we will be available to listen during a significant moment.

Special Time

When we do prioritize moments to intentionally focus on our relationships with our children, practicing special time is one of the best ways we can make the most of it. Special time can mean setting aside 20 minutes per day to remove distractions, get on the floor or sit at the table with our kids, and play. We let our kids lead us, refrain from using any judgment statements (good or bad), and spend time doing what they want to do. As opposed to a *time-out*, when you intentionally remove your attention for bad behavior, it's a *time-in* with your child, when you intentionally focus on your child and your child alone.

This doesn't have to be complicated. When your child is a baby, this may be as simple as you getting on your hands and knees next to his activity mat. When he's a toddler, it can literally mean playing with toys on the floor. Set a timer, turn your phone off — make this time only about you and your child. As your children get older, floor time can morph into mommy–son dates to the coffee shop or mommy–daughter dates to the pool. When we remove the distractions of the outside world and focus just on our children for discrete periods of time they can count on, we build a foundation of memories and mindfulness, ultimately building resilience and connection.

Weeknights and Weekends

It's tempting to phone it in with our families when we get home from work or make it to the weekends. Have you ever driven up to your house after a long day at the office, parked in the driveway, and then let out a heavy sigh as you thought

Special Time Ideas

For Preschool Kids

- Coloring, drawing, painting
- Trip to the local park
- Backyard picnic or tea party
- Reading
- Sidewalk chalk
- Vegetable garden planting
- Pretend beauty shop
- Water play with measuring cups and bowls
- Indoor/outdoor scavenger hunt

For Elementary School Kids

- Pottery painting, drawing, painting
- Bike ride around the neighborhood
- Gardening
- Sunset watching, stargazing
- Board games, puzzles, card games
- Backyard camping trip with s'mores and tent
- Daisy chains at the local park
- Baking or cooking together
- Reading at home or the local bookstore
- Home karaoke or dance party

For Preadolescents and Adolescents

- Coffee shop breakfast, lunch, or dinner date
- Drive to the beach, woods, or lake for overnight or day trip

(continued)

Special Time Ideas (*continued*)

- • Local hike or run
- • Online or in-person class together
- • Volunteer together
- • Reading together
- • Board games, card games
- • Baking or cooking together

about rejoining your kids? Sometimes, whether we like to admit it or not, it's easier to show up emotionally at work than it is to show up emotionally at home, especially when we're tired or if our kids are going through an especially rough developmental phase.

Consider taking a few minutes before you walk inside your home to reset, letting the hours that came before you fade into the background as you prepare to greet your kids and spend time with them. Maybe that hesitation to leave your car is there for a reason. It's a reminder you need to take a beat before you move on to your next commitment. When we arrive home even a little more rested and ready to parent, we're better at the task.

When the weekend arrives, commit to simplicity. Don't overschedule yourself or your kids. Leave opportunity and time for spontaneity. Choose family activities that encourage play, adventure, or discovery when possible. Avoid stacking games, errands, and appointments when you can. Although it's true that you can't always choose when your daughter's soccer games occur, you can choose to sign her up only for soccer, versus soccer *and* dance *and* piano *and* gymnastics, all in the same season. Resist the urge to squeeze in so many activities over the weekend that you and your kids are run ragged by the time Sunday night rolls around. Remember, the best parts of life usually happen in the in-between moments and downbeats, when we're taking it slow.

Need a Break

I'm all for finding contentment wherever life finds us, in using mindfulness to appreciate the beauty of right where we are instead of wistfully wasting our lives away on what we'd rather be doing or need to be doing, but, sometimes, having a family happy place can get us through some pretty rough patches. I have 2 magical family happy places seared in my mind that my brain flips to on a regular basis.

In the first one, I'm lying in a hammock in the woods. It's me and my baby daughter. We're giggling and softly swaying as we look up at the blue sky and the pine trees. The sound of car radio music wafts through the air from our camp-site, where my husband swirls up iced tea and plates turkey burgers and fruit salad.

In the second, I'm snuggled in my bed with my husband and my 2 kids. We took a day off work. School's out. We're playing Stevie Wonder on our Bluetooth speaker. The sheets and the covers feel so soft and snuggly. It's raining outside and peaceful inside. We'll probably make waffles at some point. We have nowhere else to be, nothing else to do. We're just here, with our people, in our home.

Snuggling up in my bed is completely realistic. I could have a 4-peas-in-a-pod moment most weekends with my 2 girls and my husband if I made it a priority. It just probably won't be as prolonged or as peaceful as I'd like. Inevitably, one of my kids will complain that the other one is taking up too much room, the other one will steal half the covers, my husband will realize the waffle maker is broken, and World War III will break out between my kids as we decide over alternatives like pancakes or French toast.

Swinging on a hammock with my kids on a camping trip takes more effort to achieve but is worth pursuing. Sometimes we need to physically remove ourselves from our day-to-day lives.

Vacations—even if they're in our backyards or on our apartment patios—matter to our kids. Toys and stuff can't even come close. Plus, getting away—not necessarily to a foreign country or to an island, but to just about anywhere that promotes relaxation, communication, and maybe a little boredom—matters for families too. Time off not only allows us to take a step back from the drone of life, it also allows us to explore new places, to make new memories, and to simplify—together. Time off is also an amazing way to model self-care and to get out of our day-to-day grind. This doesn't have to drain your bank account.

Now, can vacations also be stressful and annoying? Of course. Don't plan a super-complicated, 5-week adventure with your 3-year-old (if you do and you complain about it to me, I will only say I told you so). Commit instead to age-appropriate vacations, and plan for what can go wrong, when possible, realizing you won't be able to control everything all the time.

෨෨෨෨

My friend, Jeanne, a business coach and an all-around amazing working mom, puts prioritizing family time into perspective so well: "I often ask my clients to imagine they are in their 80s looking back on their lives. What do they want to say about it? What would they regret? What priorities and values do they want to say they lived by? ... When I'm older and look back at my life and look around the room, [here's] what I want to see: family and friends. True connection is what actually matters."

We live in a world where overdoing it is the norm and where taking a break is often seen as a sign of weakness.

We've got it all wrong if we buy into that rhetoric. Take time for a special adventure with your family. You don't just want, you need, to create some happy places for your family—places you'll remember when your kids are grown; memories you can access on your hardest days; moments that will, in the end, be the best ones of your life.

Looking Beyond Our Kids' Behaviors to Their True Selves

Special adventures meet some of our deepest needs as families and as mothers for real connection. When it comes to our kids, sometimes those deeper needs present themselves as bad behavior or acting out. I know it well from personal experience. Three years ago at this time, I was really worried. My daughter, bless her soul, started having some major outbursts, and I didn't know why. Tantrum after toddler tantrum, day after day, night after night, we watched her go from absolute sweetheart one minute to a total meltdown at the drop of a hat. She wouldn't eat and started shying away from school, dance, and friends—all things she had previously loved. We thought there was something seriously wrong.

It took over a month to figure out what was going on. After weeks of tears on our part and hers, we finally got a handle on the issue. In the end, it turned out she had a severe case of *pinworms*. She also had an exaggerated dread of potty training that culminated in a huge mess of a situation (I am going to spare you the details because even I gagged a little when it all went down).

The point is, I spent a lot of time last year racking my brain as to what was happening to the sensitive little soul who lives in my house. She had always been unique, but this was on a whole different level, even for her. In that month, there were nights I stayed awake feeling scared that my little girl was not ever going to be the same as she once was, and a whole lot of time I spent missing her "true self."

It came to my mind the other day as we were driving home from a fun adventure at grandma's house. I looked back in my rearview window and saw her quietly humming along, looking out at the leafy trees passing by her car window. It was the perfect picture of peace and contentment. It brought me back to that aha moment when we eventually figured out what was (literally) bugging her so much. To the grateful look in her eyes when we finally explained what was keeping her up all night and what had made her act like a completely different person. To that huge wave of relief I saw passing over her as she listened to us say that, if she took some medicine, she would be herself again.

The car ride also was a good reminder to look for her real self in the relatively common moments she still, as a function of her age or her circumstances (tired, anxious, missing a snack), goes back intermittently to that scary state. It can be easy for us to forget when our children are acting out of sorts that they may have a very good reason for it, that there is something we need to detective out (or wait out), that their real selves have gone hiding.

I know I'm not alone on this. It's true for the parents of the wayward, rebellious adolescent who one day "snaps out" of the angry teenage phase. It's true for the mom of the suddenly inconsolable 6-month-old who eventually pops a tooth. We all deal with the feeling that our kids are not themselves sometimes. It tempts us to forget the core of who they really are. We get scared that the phase will never pass, that this could be our new normal.

In our family, we learned a lot that year about how to get mindful and about how to get outside help when we needed it. (Note: if you are in a situation where you really can't figure out what's going on with your child, ask your doctor for help so he or she can come alongside you to rule out anything major.) We also learned about giving grace when we're not at our best as well. We understood better in the end about trying to see every one of the people we come in contact with as products of nature (the genes we're born with, the way we're wired) *and* nurture (the product of the environmental stressors or positives that surround us).

Dealing With the Root Cause of Your Kids' Behaviors First

Yeah, yeah, sometimes there's something major going on for my child, you say, but a lot of times he's just, well, hard to deal with because he's 3 (or 4 or 5). I feel you. Understanding child development, as well as age-appropriate sleep and exercise recommendations, is important. (Please see "Amount of Sleep Recommended to Promote Optimal Health" table later in the chapter). Getting enough sleep on a regular basis contributes not only to improved emotional regulation and behavior but also to better attention, learning, memory, quality of life, and mental and physical health. Make sure to turn off all screens 30 minutes before your child's bedtime, and don't let him have a television, computer, or other screen in his bedroom. Develop a consistent bedtime routine, including brushing his teeth, reading, and going to bed at the same time each night.

Amount of Sleep Recommended to Promote Optimal Health	
Age	Recommended Sleep per 24 Hours
4–12 months	12–16 hours (including naps)
1–2 years	11–14 hours (including naps)
3–5 years	10–13 hours (including naps)
6–12 years	9–12 hours
13–18 years	8–10 hours

Data were derived from American Academy of Pediatrics. AAP supports childhood sleep guidelines. HealthyChildren.org. Published June 13, 2016. Accessed November 13, 2020. https://www.healthychildren.org/English/news/Pages/AAP-Supports-Childhood-Sleep-Guidelines.aspx

The American Academy of Pediatrics recommends that all children have time for physical activity each day to help them prevent health issues like obesity, heart disease, and diabetes. (See "Physical Activities by Age" table later in the chapter.) Increased focus in school, improved sleep, diffused stress, and improved self-esteem are all additional benefits of consistent exercise.

Not every behavioral outburst can be accounted for by a helminth infestation or even by some major catastrophe, but, even in the smaller, less dramatic moments with our kids, it pays to think beyond the surface behaviors they're exhibiting to the deeper reasons for them.

Working mom Jessica had to remind herself of that philosophy recently. Her 4-year-old son was in some type of angry zone, upset at the world, mad at everyone. He woke up on the wrong side of the bed—again—and they wound up in some spiral tug-of-war of wills. Sobbing, he screamed and refused to brush his teeth—she could handle all that. Then he threw a small book at his baby brother, hitting him in the back and leaving a mark. Jessica felt herself almost lose it. She couldn't handle the toddler tantrum.

When someone, even someone you love, intentionally hurts your baby, the feeling that surfaces is rage. Jessica had never felt that way toward her own son until the book incident. It was a feeling of confusion, of desperation. A feeling that she must be doing this mom thing all wrong.

Her initial gut reaction? To scream, to be mean back, and to move immediately to punishment. It's not the picture of a perfect mother, but it turns out Jessica is not perfect—she is human. She thankfully remembered at that moment that her son is not perfect either. He is so much more than his toddler tantrum. Well, actually, a little song started playing in Jessica's head that helped remind her.

Physical Activities by Age

Infants	Toddlers	Preschoolers	Elementary Students	Middle Schoolers	Teenagers
Tummy time while awake	Neighborhood walks or free play outside	Tumbling, throwing, and catching	Free play and organized sports focused on fun	Activities that encourage socialization. Avoid specializing in one sport.	Activities that encourage socialization and competition, when appropriate
30+ minutes throughout day	3+ hours throughout day	3+ hours a day, including 1 hour of moderate to vigorous activity	60+ minutes of activity most days. Muscle/bone strengthening activities 3 times a week.	60+ minutes of activity most days. Muscle/bone strengthening 3 times a week.	60+ minutes of activity most days. Muscle/bone strengthening 3 times a week.

Adapted from *AAP News* Parent Plus. Making physical activity a way of life: AAP policy explained. HealthyChildren.org. Updated August 5, 2020. Accessed November 13, 2020. https://www.healthychildren.org/English/healthy-living/fitness/Pages/Making-Fitness-a-Way-of-Life.aspx

"People make bad choices if they're mad or scared or stressed. But throw a little love their way, and you'll bring out their best. True love brings out their best."

Sound eerily familiar? Yep, the *Frozen* soundtrack was her saving grace at that moment (she knew that movie would be good for something one day). Seriously, as cheesy as it may sound, that tune has it exactly right when it comes to early childhood behavior and successful parenting. It's the crux of emotion coaching and of collaborative problem-solving: an assumption that all people want to do and be their best but that traumas, circumstances, skill deficits, and developmental immaturities keep them from it a lot of the time. It's an understanding that our most important parenting goal should be to coach our kids toward desired behaviors, not to punish them for their ineptitudes.

Think about it this way: if you were in charge of a beginning-level soccer team and 1 player hadn't eaten breakfast, leaving him without any energy, and he couldn't run down the field, would you get mad at him, or would you feed him? If he missed a goal, would you sit him out of the game, or would you work on his kicking skills? If he had an incomplete pass, would you run over in the middle of the game and explain in an irritated voice how he failed, or would you use the next practice to build his skills? Storming onto the field in a fit of anger would not only be inappropriate, it would be ludicrous.

When you are a good coach, you think about where your player is going, not where the player is now. You work with the player toward the goals you share, and you consider it your role to teach and guide. We have to think about our parenting in the same goal-oriented way if we want to be successful.

Does that mean we just let our kids run free and wild, hurting others along the way, with no accountability? Not at all. Does that mean we bend to every unhealthy request our kids make? Not in the least. Do we never get angry or upset?

Tips and Tricks for Handling Early Childhood Behavioral Challenges

Age	Behavioral Challenges	Solutions
1–2 years old	● Making sense of the world by exploring ● Learning cause and effect ● Biting, hitting, or pinching to express excitement or frustration	● Childproof your home so your baby has a safe place to test things out and discover without interruptions. ● Teach her to express herself verbally versus acting out physically in anger or frustration. ● Be positive when she learns a new skill or realizes her actions cause something to happen. ● Offer toys that teach about size, shape, and color, like nesting toys, stacking blocks, and common kitchen containers. ● Distract and redirect whenever possible. ● Use the word no judiciously. ● Celebrate experiments and excitement as she discovers the world.
2–3 years old	● Realizing is separate individual from parents and caregivers ● Likely to assert himself ● Likely to communicate likes and dislikes ● Wants to act independently	● Talk about feelings. ● Offer ideas for how to manage strong emotions. ● Empathize. ● Use visual aids when he needs to wait or has to be patient (like a timer or a stop sign).

(continued)

Tips and Tricks for Handling Early Childhood Behavioral Challenges (*continued*)

Age	Behavioral Challenges	Solutions
2-3 years old (*continued*)	● Still developing language skills to help express ideas, wants, and needs ● Still learning to understand logic ● Hard time with waiting and self-control	● Let him make as many age-appropriate choices as possible. ● Practice self-control by playing turn-taking games and using pretend play.
4-5 years old	● Increasing independence ● Able to tell fantasy from real life ● Wants to be like friends ● Wants to please ● Demanding at times, cooperative at times	● Praise desirable behaviors and give less attention to undesirable actions. ● Be consistent with limit setting and discipline from all caregivers. ● Stick to a regular sleep, activity, eating, and exercise schedule. ● Give choices whenever possible. ● Use a warm, loving, but firm tone when redirection is needed.

That's impossible. It does mean that we first think of our children as fellow people, who usually act out based on feelings and needs, not spite. It means

● **We remember that, in 99% of cases, our children's behaviors do not constitute emergencies.** There is almost always time to stop, get ourselves peaceful, and then move to action.

● **We reality check our deepest fears and disappointments.** In those whirlwind moments of parenting, the fears that we've been storing down in the depths make their way to the forefront of our minds quite often. But fears like, "My child doesn't have a bone of empathy in her body," or, "My kids will never love each other," while seemingly real in the moment, are hardly ever based in reality. Remember, aiming for perfectly behaved kids is unrealistic and unfair. We can't let our fears dictate our in-the-moment parenting responses.

● **We own our own emotions and role model healthy ways to deal with those feelings that rise to the surface when we're triggered.** It's perfectly OK to say to your child, "Mommy feels disappointed and angry right now. I need to take a second to calm down." In fact, when we consistently acknowledge what's going on for us inside and demonstrate how to deal with the raw feelings we have in nonviolent, nonharmful ways, we are showing our kids how they can do the same.

● **We teach kids to label their emotions.** We point out that "Jayda is frustrated she can't play with that toy right now," or "Owen is sad he can't have an ice cream today," so our kids learn to recognize how they're feeling, a first step in dealing with those emotions.

● **We set firm limits and rules about what is OK and what is not.** When our kids use inappropriate methods to express their emotions and get their needs met, we help them find an alternative solution. "We don't hit. Can you think of another option?" We use authoritative parenting.

- **We use time-outs sparingly and natural consequences wisely.** A book to the back of a sibling? In my house, that is a line we don't cross. However, time-outs don't have to be angry, dragged out power struggles. They can be a chance to help kids stop and get control of themselves. If we do set a consequence for an action, we make it logical and realistic (like taking away a privilege or helping to clean up a mess that was made), not far-fetched or punitive for the whole family—"That's it! No playdates for a month!"

- **We allow, whenever possible, our children to brainstorm their own solutions.** "You'll need your hair brushed before we can leave. You want to keep playing right now. What should we do?"

Our kids are so often trying their hardest but coming up against factors they just cannot control or understand themselves. It's up to us as parents to help them navigate, to give them the space and support they need, and to love them no matter what. We need to believe that their true selves are just waiting to be found. We need to understand that, sometimes, we just need to look in their less obvious hiding places to find them.

Listening to Our Kids' Needs

Sometimes those hiding places are under beds. I came home at 1:00 pm on a Saturday last week after working at my clinic, ready to play and to be present. I was hoping that I'd be met with excitement and energy. Instead, my littlest girl was in complete disarray. She was sitting under her bed when I walked in, fully dressed in her mermaid costume with a jeweled crown and black, glossy rain boots. She was sobbing.

"I don't want to go!" she screamed when I walked through the door.

Authoritative Parenting: An Evidence-Based Approach

Parents who practice an authoritative parenting style with their children balance warmth and support with firm limits.

Children raised with authoritative parenting are more likely to be resilient and less likely to engage in risky behaviors.

Kenneth R. Ginsburg, MD, MS Ed, FAAP, described this well-studied, effective approach in his book, *Building Resilience in Children and Teens: Giving Kids Roots and Wings*. He calls it *balanced* or *lighthouse* parenting.

"This parent sets reasonable limits, expects good behavior, offers a lot of love, and encourages kids to make choices and be independent, but when it comes to the big issues, it's, 'Do as I say.'"

"Oh, hello, little angel child," I thought to myself.

We were supposed to attend a housewarming party for one of our friends an hour later and she had been acting up about going for the past 3 hours while she waited for me to return from work. For about 20 minutes, I tried to convince her that we would all be together there, that it would be fun, that she would be happy. But, when we finally had everyone in the house dressed and ready to go (which seemed like an eternity later), she was still in toddler tantrum mode and kept talking about how she just could not do it.

I had a decision to make. I could push her to do the thing I wanted her to do so I could fulfill all of my social obligations, or I could listen to what she was asking for. On the surface, it felt like I would be giving in to her by not going along with my original plans. There are definitely times I know I need to stick to my guns despite her loud protests otherwise (like when she wants brownies for dinner or when she doesn't feel like going to school). Most times that's the case, actually. Other times, though, I can tell we're in a different zone.

After all that time spent reassuring her, I stopped to listen to what she was really telling me: I miss you and I want to spend time with you—just you. Will you please give me your undivided attention for a few hours?

My husband and I talked by ourselves. We made sure that my daughter was in control of herself (some deep breathing while she counted to 10). I sat her down and let her know it was Daddy and I deciding what we were doing today and we decided it would be better for everyone if her older sister and Daddy represented us at the party. Then, I gave her a few activity choices for our time together. I was *not* about to be swindled into some ice cream sundae escapade.

We ended up spending 4 amazing hours together, just the 2 of us. We went to the park and had a mommy–daughter lunch date. Then we came home and read books all snuggled up on the porch. The crazy thing? I was nervous at first that she might take her "win" on our day's activities as an opportunity to walk all over me. But she was the most well-behaved, grateful toddler ever for the whole outing.

Even more amazing? When I took the time to treat her like an actual human who had real needs (like *all* of us have), she spent the whole evening running around the house doing imaginary play in that mermaid outfit, entertained almost entirely by her dolls. She was almost annoyed when I asked if I could jump in to play.

"Uh, I'm really playing with my mermaid friends, Mom."

Okaaaay. Wow. It was a 180° change. Yep, by attending to her very sincere request for attention, by giving her the time she deserved, I was the one who lucked out *the entire rest of the day*. It blew my mind. It will for you too, if you take a moment to consider if there is some underlying issue going on when your child is acting particularly "needy." Maybe he needs more rest or to get his body moving. Or, maybe, he simply needs some more special time with you.

Managing Our Kids' Big Emotions (and Our Own)

The weekend I packed up all my belongings, cleaned out my house, and hauled everything across town while we set up camp for 1 year at my parents' house in an effort to pay off all that remaining student loan debt was a memorable one.

They say moving is one of the most stressful life events—right up there with getting married and starting a new job. I knew parts of it would be rough when we made our decision to go all out on debt repayment, but I also knew we had to make a major shift in our financial plan if we wanted to ever feel a little freer. Once we signed on the dotted line, there was a lot to do to make it all happen, from arranging cleaners to buying moving supplies and getting everything packed up in time.

I wasn't trying to type A myself through that major life change, but I sure was good at it. I made the checklists. I checked off all the boxes. It felt good to be organized. Even so, 2 months after accepting our tenants, making child care shifts, and getting everything else arranged in a logical manner, it all hit me full force emotionally.

It hit my kids too.

All their toys were in boxes, and half the rooms in our house became off-limits that last week to accommodate drying touch-up paint. My girls tried their best for about 2 hours the morning their playroom was cordoned off to find something else to do. The fix-it guy maneuvered around them, trying to avoid their antics as I unsuccessfully encouraged them to get creative. Then one of my girls hit some kind of behavioral limit. A shoe was thrown. Some hair was pulled. There was an all-out screaming event held by the toddler. She should have charged admission it was so dramatic.

I piled them in the car, understanding full well that kids sometimes express their frustrations and stress in less than ideal ways.

"Let's go to the berry farm," I said, imagining myself peacefully meandering through rows of blueberry bushes with a wagon of equally serene children behind me. "We can grab some lunch on the way."

The kids were ecstatic, ready to spend a more enjoyable afternoon with a less distracted mom. We stopped at our favorite burrito bowl place, adding 3 lemonades to the order just because. I could feel the mood lift, my littlest now happily skipping along, holding my hand. She swung herself up onto my arm, making monkey noises as she attempted to climb me. The drink carrier tipped as I tried to set it down on the sidewalk so I could rearrange my crew and our food. Off we went again, past the shops and other families enjoying their days.

I'd almost made it to the car when the first lemonade fell out of the carrier, tumbling to the ground as my daughter tried again to use my body as a jungle gym, despite my admonishments. I set the carrier on the hood, presumably safe from mishap while I strapped everyone into their car seats and took a big breath.

I let my guard down too soon, though. The second lemonade made its downward turn as it slid across the wet hood, exploding like a yellow bomb as it hit the pavement. I grabbed the carrier just before the final cup met its demise, only to have the lid flip off when I tried to set it into my cup holder. Before I could catch it, a sweet, sticky film covered the console. It splashed onto the passenger seat and down to the floorboards.

Lemonade was everywhere. *Everywhere.* I felt a low, guttural sound come from somewhere around my mid-chest. And then I felt myself start to cry.

This was not a controlled, adult, tears around my eyes kind of sniffle. It was a full-on, body shaking, sobbing into my steering wheel kind of cry—the kind that makes your kids really quiet, the kind that makes you really quiet after 5 seconds because you realize you are surrounded only by the sound of silence. It was only spilled lemonade, but somehow it meant more.

"Mommy, why are you crying?" my oldest whispered.

"Yeah, mom, only kids are supposed to cry," I heard my baby girl quip.

"No, mommies can cry," she responded. "Especially when they're having a hard day. Mommy is having a hard day. All of her lemonade spilled, and it ruined the car. And we're moving, Sissy. Moving can be very hard."

"Oh, yeah," she answered back. "It's OK for adults to cry about that. Don't worry, Mommy, it will be all right."

I sat listening to my very young children have a very grown-up conversation about the way life works as I pulled myself together. I looked back at them, feeling a little sheepish that the only adult in the car was having the most difficulty being wise. I saw their earnest faces smiling back at me and I remembered this truth: Our children learn just as much from our real emotions, from our in-the-moment mistakes, even from our flat-out parenting failures, as they do from the scripted, controlled learning experiences we arrange or manipulate for them. When they see us being vulnerable about the way we feel, they can be honest about the way they feel too.

Now that I was a bit more composed, I explained myself:

"You know, Mommy is really excited about our move and what that's going to mean for our family—that we're working on a goal to spend more time together and to be stronger as a team. You're right, though. All the little parts and pieces that have to come together to make this move happen are sometimes overwhelming. Those lemonades falling—one after another—was what they call 'the straw that broke the camel's back.' Every once in a while, your body needs you to just let your emotions out a little so they don't keep getting bottled up. When you least expect it, sometimes the kettle lets off a little steam. Just like that happens for you guys sometimes, it happens for Mommy too."

I watched their little heads nod, like old sages. My kids are not always that attentive, but, in that moment, they sure were. I had a captive audience, maybe because I shocked them a bit with my sobfest but, hopefully, also because they truly know that feelings are OK.

They know they're loved no matter what their emotions, however mixed up they feel. They know it's all right to work through all the complex feelings that come with making big changes. They know it's OK for things to be not all bad, not all good, but somewhere in between. When you are authentic with your kids, they learn that authenticity is something to be desired.

Now, let's not take this too far. I'm not suggesting you let your kids in on every deep, dark emotion you ever have, or that you overshare your mental play-by-play on a regular basis. Obviously, sobbing through our days is neither productive nor healthy for our children. What I am suggesting is this: it's important to let our kids learn how to be strong and brave, to get past their fears, to build resilience. It's equally important that they learn how to be vulnerable.

I'm suggesting we show them that when they're weak, they're still lovable—that they're still strong, even when they don't feel like they are—that accepting and working through our emotions is another form of developing that all important grow-from-your-struggles skill, that they're part of a community that loves them no matter what.

The dinner table replay of the day's events was pretty epic that evening, but what was most impressive was the way my kids jumped in as I summarized the story to my husband. He sat there wide-eyed as I recounted the tumbling drinks, the lemonade bath, and the crazy conversation that ensued.

"Mommy lost her marbles a little bit this afternoon," I laughed to my husband.

The toddler piped up quickly as she slurped her noodles off the fork. "Yeah, but we helped her find them again."

Yes, baby girl, I thought. *You sure did.*

Dealing With Our Culture of Screens and Devices

Listening to our emotions and to our kids' emotions is a good thing, but I'm not prescribing that we let our feelings drive all our behaviors, especially when it comes to screens and devices. Our culture of immediacy and convenience makes it exceedingly difficult to *not* give in to our kids' demands, even when they're unhealthy.

Case in point last week in my friend Anne's kitchen. One of her kids was hoisting herself halfway onto the counter and reached for a pen against the wall. On her way down, she bumped her elbow, hitting right on her funny bone. She burst into tears. That wasn't the scary part.

Here's what really shook Anne up. As her daughter let out her first wail and rounded into a ball in the floor, the first words out of her mouth were, "Mama, can I watch a show?"

Seriously, like mid-scream, the absolute first thing that came into her mind was not physical comfort or emotional support, or even some verbal proclamation of pain. It was *television*.

She's never had that kind of Pavlov's dog reaction before to an injury, and, at first, Anne kind of brushed it off, but then she started thinking more and more about her daughter's relationship with screens and about our current culture of quick-fix distractions and personalized, immediate conveniences. She also started thinking about the ways she chose to spend time she could be connecting with her daughter. She realized how many times she had given her daughter other nonproductive ways to amuse herself so Anne could get stuff done herself.

It would have been tempting to blame the TV—the device itself—for Anne's daughter's behavior that day. She can't count the number of times she's heard the recommendations from her pediatrician about limiting the total amount of time per day kids use their screens or heard suggestions about caring equally about content versus total screen time. Families like Anne's seem to understand that too much and the wrong kind of screen use is bad for their kids. This, though, was a different part of the technology revolution she'd never even stopped to consider: Not only was she letting her child be entertained by screens, she was letting her child be comforted by screens too. The screen was a proxy for a bigger, societal problem.

We live in a world where it has become incredibly difficult to say no to our children because we have so many ways we can say yes. Over the first postmillennial decade, the cultural norms around how we navigate our daily tasks have so dramatically changed. There's increasing pressure on parents to have 1,000 convenient—but unhelpful—ways to keep our kids happy. The "tech culture of convenience" has rewoven the task of raising children.

"Our culture, in large part, has been influenced by the technological revolution—a series of amazing advancements that have modernized everything from shopping to scheduling doctors' appointments. But has it all been for the better? It turns out kids who grew up with the technological coming of age (typically born in the early 2000s—the iGen kids or Gen Y kids)—are struggling as a result of it," said Kristin Valerius, PhD, a Portland, OR, child psychologist and director of Sundstrom Clinical Services, when I sat down with her to dive deep on the subject.

The research backs her up. First of all, it shows heavy childhood screen use is ubiquitous. According to Jean M.

Twenge, MD, a psychologist and researcher, in her 2017 article in *The Atlantic*:

> ...members of this generation are growing up with smartphones, have an Instagram account before they start high school, and do not remember a time before the internet. The Millennials grew up with the web as well, but it wasn't ever-present in their lives, at hand at all times, day and night. iGen's oldest members were early adolescents when the iPhone was introduced, in 2007, and high-school students when the iPad entered the scene, in 2010. A 2017 survey of more than 5,000 American teens found that three out of four owned an iPhone.

Dr Twenge has been analyzing adolescents' levels of happiness and well-being across generations for more than 25 years using the Monitoring the Future survey. The survey, conducted since the mid-'70s, asks 8th, 10th, and 12th graders about their self-esteem, life satisfaction, and daily activities like tech use. Kids, of course, have always had fluctuations in happiness from year to year, but in 2012 something astonishing happened: well-being dropped off dramatically. Not just a little drop-off. Like, drop off a cliff drop-off, and it stayed that way. After 20 years of relative stability in overall happiness, life satisfaction, and self-esteem, it went downhill fast...and never recovered. It didn't matter the kids' financial situations; they—across the board—seemed to be having a harder time.

"In all my analyses of generational data—some reaching back to the 1930s—I had never seen anything like it," Dr Twenge said.

Of course, no single event, including the advent of pervasive, individualized technology, defines a generation. But the dual increase in mental health concerns and media use seem to be strongly connected. We know that factors like heavy social media use, texting, computer games, and accessing the internet are not the keys to a teen's happiness. In fact, studies show heavy screen use is actually associated with decreased happiness, whereas things like sports and in-person social interactions are associated with improved life satisfaction.

What happened in 2012? Technology with its apps, and devices, and new ways of doing everything became fully infiltrated, that's what happened. At the end of 2012, the year of the huge drop-off, the proportion of Americans who owned a smartphone surpassed 50%. In an April 8, 2015, article, the Pew Research Center, Internet and Tech, stated that by 2015, the percentage of iGen youth with smartphones was 73%, up from 37% in 2013. The changes Dr Twenge saw were not based on ethnicity or on social-economic status or on suburban or rural location. Across the board, no matter what their demographics, teens suddenly were living on their smartphones.

"I don't think [we have a problem] just because so many kids are on their devices," says Dr Valerius. "If that were the case, then just taking the phone would solve it—but that doesn't. I believe device usage is a proxy measure for how ubiquitous the individualized convenient way of doing things had become. And in reweaving the task, our parenting job became harder, our kids missed out on important developmental tasks, so that by the time these iGen were teenagers circa 2012, they were showing the stress fractures of growing up in this Brave New Tech World."

Everyone talks about how TV is bad, that devices are bad, and that's important, but it also misses the point. By focusing on device use, we keep parents focused (and yelling at their kids) for how often they are on that device instead of focusing them on how many ways they need to help their kids navigate life…and it keeps parents' focus away from themselves and why they are feeling so much pressure to just satisfy their kids at every moment.

When we allow technology (and any other knee-jerk easy solutions) to soothe and entertain our kids, we replace patience with immediacy, we limit our kids' abilities to deal with negative emotions on their own, and we give quick-fix, personalized solutions to boredom, reducing our children's abilities to handle less stimulating environments. We take away the opportunity to develop grit.

As a working mom, my family time is limited throughout the week. In the evenings, I'm tired. On the weekends, I'm always hoping for reduced stress, but with 2 little ones in tow, that's hardly ever the case. Nothing is worse than coming home from an exhausting day at work only to be inundated with tears and squabbling and strife. It's extremely hard for modern, stressed-out families to "just say no" to letting screens parent our kids in the name of peace and harmony, but I firmly believe that we have to be fully aware of our choices if we want our children to be resilient and our parenting to be successful.

How Do We Manage Screens and Mitigate Their Use?

We Model Good Screen Use Behavior Ourselves

Kids do what they see. That includes teenagers. If mom and dad are texting and scrolling all day, their kids will want to too. Sometimes we have to be on our devices, but, when we can, we should limit our own use.

We Deepen Our Connection With Our Kids

In this modern world, we have to create space to more deeply connect with our kids. It's not going to happen on its own. We have to be intentional about it. Mealtimes, bedtimes, outings, holiday rituals—when we focus on using these moments as ways to build community and connection, we glean their true value. Connectedness helps with emotional regulation, self-soothing, and other skills that are lacking from our children's digital experience.

We Help Our Children Build a Network of People Who Know Them, Including Their Weaknesses

"True relationship and intimacy come from vulnerably failing and then reconciling, not from being fake or perfect all the time," says Dr Valerius. "When you let your kids experience that kind of transparent connection with others, they learn that they have value no matter what, that they don't have to be perfect to be loved."

We Learn to Value Negative Emotions and Failure in Our Kids and in Ourselves

It's not our job to make sure our kids are always happy or even to make sure they're perfectly well-behaved. It is our job to make sure we teach them to trust they will be OK when happiness comes and goes. How do we do that? We let our kids be bored and uncertain about how to fill their free time. The creativity and problem-solving that happen in that bored space are crucial for the sort of coping that they will have to do throughout their adolescence.

We let our kids be upset occasionally, we let them work through disappointments (à la my lemonade fiasco), we allow them to experience things not going their way early on so that, years down the road, they can handle life's curveballs with more grace and perspective.

We Limit Tech Use

Of course, letting our kids be bored—given that we could instantly take it away—means that their whining and pestering also fills that space. Constantly. And any good modern mommy has times that they cave just to have a moment of peace. That's where these American Academy of Pediatrics recommendations come in.

American Academy of Pediatrics Screen Time Recommendations

- Avoid digital media use (except video-chatting) in children younger than 18 to 24 months.
- For children ages 18 to 24 months, if you want to introduce digital media, choose high-quality programming and use media together with your child. Avoid solo media use in this age group.
- Do not feel pressured to introduce technology early; interfaces are so intuitive that children will figure them out quickly once they start using them at home or in school.
- For children 2 to 5 years of age, limit screen use to 1 hour per day of high-quality programming, coview with your children, help children understand what they are seeing, and help them apply what they learn to the world around them.
- Avoid fast-paced programs (young children do not understand them as well), apps with lots of distracting content, and any violent content.
- Turn off televisions and other devices when not in use.
- Avoid using media as the only way to calm your child. Although there are intermittent times (eg, medical procedures, airplane flights) when media is useful as a soothing strategy, there is concern that using media as strategy to calm could lead to problems with limit setting or the inability of children to develop their own emotion regulation. Ask your pediatrician for help if needed.
- Monitor children's media content and what apps are used or downloaded. Test apps before the child

(continued)

American Academy of Pediatrics Screen Time Recommendations (*continued*)

uses them, play together, and ask the child what he or she thinks about the app.

• Keep bedrooms, mealtimes, and parent-child play-times screen free for children and parents. Parents can set a "do not disturb" option on their phones during these times.

• No screens 1 hour before bedtime, and remove devices from bedrooms before bed.

From American Academy of Pediatrics Council on Communications and Media. Media and young minds. *Pediatrics*. 2016;138(5):e20162591 PMID: 27940793 https://doi.org/10.1542/peds.2016-2591

Feeling defeated already as you read this? Don't. First, realize that the way modern moms are often tempted to deal with their kids' incessant begging to have whatever they need is not some type of character flaw—it's a product of our kids' environments: a world where personalization, convenience, and entitlement surrounds them.

"I truly believe the begging is harder to withstand for us than it was for our mothers because they couldn't say yes and we can," says Dr Valerius. "Standing firm seems to be an impossible task sometimes for the parents of patients I see—and for myself at times. If we don't get connected with the task and the emotions it stirs up in us, it doesn't matter what tech limits we know we *should* have…we will take a path of lesser resistance."

Limiting Our Own Distractions

Our kids' device use is one thing, but what about our own? As more and more studies emerge about the dangerous outcomes associated with screen usage, parental screen time is coming further and further to the forefront. As we learn more about the physical dangers linked to parenting with a smartphone in front of our faces at all times, the research on how parental addiction to screens affects children's cognitive development has lagged behind. In the last few years, we're starting to see more rigorous studies show just how important it is to set our phones down in the presence of our children. Erika Christakis put the dangers of parental screen time well in a 2018 article in *The Atlantic*, "The Dangers of Distracted Parenting."

> Occasional parental inattention is not catastrophic (and may even build resilience), but chronic distraction is another story. Smartphone use has been associated with a familiar sign of addiction: Distracted adults grow irritable when their phone use is interrupted; they not only miss emotional cues but actually misread them. A tuned-out parent may be quicker to anger than an engaged one, assuming that a child is trying to be manipulative when, in reality, she just wants attention. Short, deliberate separations can of course be harmless, even healthy, for parent and child alike (especially as children get older and require more independence). But that sort of separation is different than the inattention that occurs when a parent is *with* a child but communicating through his or her nonengagement that the child is less valuable than an email. A mother telling kids to go out and play, a father saying he needs to concentrate on a chore for the next half hour—these are entirely reasonable responses to the competing demands of adult life. What's going on today, however, is the rise of *unpredictable* care, governed by the beeps and enticements of smartphones. We seem to have stumbled into the worst model of parenting imaginable—always present physically, thereby blocking children's autonomy, yet only fitfully present emotionally.

Our screen time dilemmas are not going away anytime soon. Devices are here to stay—for us and for our kids—but we don't have to let them break into our homes every other second, invading our lives. With your eyes on the future, make a commitment to using screens (as much as possible) as tools instead of trespassers.

Navigating School Obligations

Figuring out how to handle screen time as a working mom can be daunting, but even more intimidating? Figuring out how to handle schooltime. How do you deal with the demands of your kid's educational environment as a working mom? How do you prioritize and invest in your child's learning, without stressing yourself and everyone else out in the process?

This is going to sound counterintuitive, but my best advice for dealing with school is to volunteer. *"Volunteer?!"* I can you feel you getting angry at me from this side of the page, but hear me out. Intermittent volunteering can make a world of difference for your relationship with your child and with your child's teacher, especially in the early years. Remember how I squeezed myself into that little chair last fall and made paper garlands? I signed up out of guilt, but I learned a lot about the value of volunteering within just a few minutes. I'm not talking every week or every field trip. I'm talking every other month (or less) in the classroom.

Your goal here is to observe your child as he interacts with the other students and with the teacher (to get the feel of what's going on in the classroom) and to develop a face-to-face relationship with your child's teacher so that, even though you only see him every once in a while, he knows you when you communicate with him at other times about your child's needs and your concerns. Let other parents who do not have full-time jobs do the hard-core school volunteer work and remember to thank them profusely for it.

When you have to make a choice, choose in-classroom volunteer opportunities over field trip opportunities. During

field trips, the kids are all jazzed about whatever they're visiting—the zoo or the museum. They're usually less excited
about sharing the new adventure with you and more excited
about sharing it with their buddies. On the other hand, when
you volunteer in the classroom, you and your child can benefit more from your efforts.

Only get as involved with school and with school administrative and fundraising activities as works well for you.
Fundraisers and PTA meetings just aren't my thing. If you're
thrilled to be invested administratively with your child's
school, you should go for it, but I know that—at this point in
my life—I don't have the time or the interest. In a few years,
there may be more space, but for now it just won't happen
without it causing resentment and overwhelm. Most working
moms I know feel the same.

Don't hesitate to use email to communicate instead of waiting for direct, face-to-face discussion opportunities with your
child's teacher. So what if it's not you at pickup every day?
You can just as easily (and probably more efficiently, to be
honest) get the lowdown on your kid's school experience by
sending your child's teacher a quick message when it works
well for you.

It is important to get to know the other kids' parents in your
child's class. It's nice to be able to call someone for clarification
on homework assignments or to check the date for library
night or when the winter play starts. No matter what your
child care situation is, sometimes things will go awry when
you are trying to manage multiple schedules. It pays to have a
few other moms' or dads' contact information in case of emergencies, but filling your address book isn't enough. A few true
friendships (or at least some solid familiarity) with other parents will make you and your child more comfortable. A good
friend will always be there when you need them to pinch-hit
when you're called by the school nurse for minor issues, like
your child's intermittent sore throat or fleeting stomachache.

Quick Tips for Staying Involved With Your Child's School Life

- Sign up for email newsletter updates from the school so you can stay up to date on major happenings.

- Designate a way to communicate with your child's teacher effectively and efficiently; apps, email, and text all work well, depending on the situation.

- Stay in the know by developing a community of other parents you know and trust.

- Sign up to volunteer only if it works for your schedule and if you have enough bandwidth to handle it.

- Ask ahead of time about special field trips and classroom events on the calendar so you can pre-plan and see which ones your works schedule will allow you to attend.

Managing Summer Breaks

Do you remember your childhood summer vacations? I remember them vividly—my brother and I running free in the backyard, creating forts at the neighbor's. My father was a teacher, making summers especially luxurious. We hardly ever went on a fancy trip, but just the fact that my dad was present—working on projects around the house or making extra money doing construction projects for family friends—made those special days seem to go on forever. Our most exciting ritual came about mid-July, when we'd go on a series of car camping trips in the California redwoods. Canned stew and spaghetti with meat sauce were almost always on the menu, along with cold cereal in the morning and PB and Js for lunch.

Even if you didn't grow up with a teacher parent, you probably did grow up feeling that sense of summer freedom—that something was different—even lazy and boring—compared to normal. That's the kind of feeling we still want to give our kids on their breaks. Most kids these days have a more structured summer than we did, with scheduled camps, activities, and playdates—especially if both of their parents are working. We can still maintain that free and easy kind of feeling for our kids during summer breaks, though—a feeling they desperately need incrementally throughout their lives—by choosing scheduled activities that foster creativity and fun over academic advancement.

Some camps are better than others. Whenever possible pick camps that get your kids outside and moving, that give them the opportunity to explore and play instead of sit and learn. Our children get enough rote memorization or fact acquisition opportunities in the school year. Summers are meant to be free. Remember, a little boredom breeds creative kids. Creative kids who know how to problem solve and to play develop into more resilient adults.

Working With Other Parents to Make a Summer Plan

Even though camps can be great ways to (can we just go ahead and say it?) occupy our children during the summer months, they can also be a huge financial drain and can create their own brand of scheduling nightmares for working parents, especially when they have later start times and earlier end times than the regular school year schedule. This is where your friendships with other parents come into play.

I'm not sure what I would do without the other moms in my posse—the women who step in for me as I try to juggle it all. I've had friends pick my kids up from camps, host playdates—even take my kids for me to lunch with their own little ones. I wish I could say that I do the same for them all the time—that I watch their kids while they work—but I can't. Every once in a while, I start to get worried about my lack of contribution to my mommy village, but then I remember the truth: I have a unique place in the circle. I may not bake all the cookies and host all the midweek get-togethers, but I sure show up for my friends when they need advice over coffee or if they're seriously worried about their kid's health. That's what a village is—not everyone doing exactly the same thing, but everyone doing the thing they can do (or have the time to do) better than anyone else.

Birthday Parties and Other Celebrations

How many kid birthday parties or other celebrations do you have on your calendar? It can be hard to figure out what events are actually worth attending, what will make a difference in the long run as you think about your child's future friendships or life experiences. The pressure to say yes to each invitation can be weighty. When planning your own events, it's equally easy to get caught up in the pressure to make them Pinterest-worthy at all costs.

My actual, real-life Pinterest board for my daughter's first birthday party was *out of control*. I even hand made little stamped tags with aqua twine and prepared a full Italian smorgasbord full of food. The party was beautiful, but I remember swearing under my breath and feeling frantic the whole weekend before the event as I tried to make it all picture perfect. For what purpose? When I analyzed my heart, I realized my intention was to make sure I appeared even more invested and present for my children than the other moms who didn't work did, even though it negatively affected my mental health and put me out financially.

After going through a few more flustered parties, I realized I needed to stop trying to Martha Stewart everything to the nth degree. I also needed to *get off Pinterest* and to focus more on the experiences I was creating over the gifts I bought or the decorations I put up. I'll be honest: there have been times as I struggled to pay off student loan debt and found myself living paycheck to paycheck that I really couldn't even afford gifts at all. To keep up with the world's expectations of what it means to show up as a mom, I overextended myself both financially and from a mental health perspective. Turning away from all that allowed me to authentically show up in a way that fit my budget and intentions better.

Listen, as working moms we have to have to be real about our motives and our obligations. We have too much on our plates to let outside pressures or pictures of what mother-hood should look like dictate our actions when it comes to childhood celebrations and demonstrations of love.

Focusing on What Matters When It Comes to Academics and After-school Activities

We all want our kids to reach their full potential. When we're working moms, though, sometimes it can seem like organizing activities and promoting academic success are extra jobs that require our full attention.

Before you get bogged down in arranging and planning academic experiences and after-school activities, make sure you get a grip on your parenting goals and philosophy. I've had to dig deep in this area time and time again. I have to check in with myself about my own motivations and goals—about what really matters. In the end, we want to raise kids who are well-adjusted, self-sufficient, resilient adults; who love what they do, no matter what that is; and who under-stand that they have to work hard to achieve their dreams. That is the *real* measure of success.

I recommend focusing on 1 or 2 weekly nonschool activ-ities per kid per season (3 maximum). Mix it up while they are young, if possible, unless they find something *they* love that they want to stick with. If you can, find one active activity and one more academic or community option (think music class, chess club, art class). For older kids, let them choose from a handful of options versus demanding that they be involved with a specific activity *you* really care about. Try to stick with whichever activity they choose through the season, and then switch it up if it's not working out so you can help foster a little perseverance and commitment.

Above all, if we want our children to be truly successful academically and professionally, we have to allow our kids to see us fail and then rebound from our own failures. Use family dinnertimes to talk about the best parts of your day and also about the challenges you faced and the ways you overcame them. Have your kids, when they are old enough, share their rose (best) and thorn (worst) of their day as well. Work on letting them figure problems out on their own, waiting to jump in with help until they ask you for it, and, even then, assisting mostly by helping them to problem solve the situation for themselves.

In your own professional development, look for ways you can adjust your attitude to consider yourself a learner. When you don't perform as well as you want to at work, use it as an opportunity to grow as opposed to looking at each mini failure as a sign of ineptitude. Approach your kids' failures in the same way. "I can't do that" is usually met with a "yet" in my house. "You can't do it yet. But did you try your best? OK, then you did a great job! You will get there."

Working mom Alejandra is an amazing painter. She tried to sell her work in galleries, but she eventually had to change course when she didn't "make it" right away in the art world. The bills started rolling in after she graduated from art school and had her first son. She likes her graphic design job, but she still dreams about pursuing a full-time painting career.

> One day I'll do it. It's just not the right time at this moment. I work in a retail store on the weekends to make ends meet. My son used to ask me why I gave up on painting, and, at first, I wanted to tell him some lie about how it's not what I really wanted to do, but then I

saw how walking him through the challenges I've faced in my professional career could be a really powerful way to help him learn how to deal with his own setbacks. I haven't given up on my dreams. I haven't failed. I'm just not there yet.

When you get involved in activities or make choices about which school or educational programs are best, look first at how they fit with the personality of your child. Does your child need a warm, supportive environment to thrive, even if it's not seemingly as rigorous as another option? It might just serve him better in the long run. Does your kid need more structure and accountability? An educational program that uses that model may work best. The temperament of your child will often determine her needs and her ability to work well within the system where she goes to learn every day.

Managing Work When Your Kids Are Sick

What's worse than navigating schedules for well kids as a working mom? Trying to manage work and logistics when they are sick. As a pediatrician, I see how completely devastating illnesses can be for moms when it comes to maintaining their own presence in the workplace. And, although sometimes kids really are so unwell that they need constant supervision and isolation to get better, a lot of times parents don't realize that there are tricks many of us pediatricians use with our own kids to get through sick season with a little more sanity.

Stay Away From Sick People

Not all illnesses are avoidable, but environmental factors do play a role. A child who goes to indoor play facilities (like a children's museum or indoor play gym) multiple times a week will be more likely to catch whatever viruses are floating around there. I'm serious—I swore off almost all enclosed shared play places during peak sick seasons once I went through one winter with my first child. Anything with "Children's" in the title is a no-go for me during the winter weeks. I'm not a shut-in; I just pick and choose activities on the basis of the scientific fact that more kids plus more germs equals more chances of your kid getting germs too. During sick season, I opt for outdoor snow activities, pottery painting studios, and smaller gatherings. Knowing full well you can never completely avoid illness, I try to at least play the odds correctly.

Be a Bit More Vigilant

There are a few basics of good health that every parent knows are important, but, if you're a working mom, these things are critical.

Wash Those Hands

Parents often spend a ton of money on fancy, cold-busting vitamins and supplements, but the best way to prevent catching most germs is free: handwashing. Teach your kids to thoroughly scrub with warm, soapy water for at least 20 seconds each time they wash and to head to the sink before meals, after using the bathroom, and after they cough or sneeze.

Keep Your Febrile Child Home

There is a (very good) reason most child care centers and schools have a policy that students should stay home if they've had a fever within the previous 24 hours: when a virus or bacteria attack the human body, fever is part of the body's attempt to fight back. Schools and care centers don't want kids hanging out in classrooms while the illness battle is still raging, as the bacteria or virus may make its way to another student in the process. Instead, use the time at home to help your child focus on fluids and rest so he can reenter care ready to learn and play.

Teach Your Child About the "Cough Pocket"

When you sneeze or cough, little virus or bacteria particles go shooting through the air (I know, science is kind of gross, but it's also kind of cool). They can travel up to 100 miles per hour. In an ideal world, kids would catch all those nasties in a tissue, but youngsters often don't have that much foresight. Be practical instead. Once she's old enough, show your child how to make a cough pocket with her elbow (coughing into the crock of her arm, like Dracula). Don't be surprised if this takes quite a bit of reinforcing. Good habits take time to ingrain.

Attend to the Basics

Our bodies avoid and fight illnesses best when they're in prime shape. Eating a healthy diet rich in vegetables, fruits, and whole grains sets kids up for health success. Give your kids plenty of exercise and water, focus on healthy sleep habits, and make sure they're up to date on all their vaccinations.

Get a Backup Plan in Place

When people ask me how I get everything done in my life— professionally, personally, when it comes to my kids— I always have a simple answer: backup. Help. Murphy's Law seems to apply even more strongly when you have multiple balls you're juggling because there are more chances for things *to go wrong.* When I hear celebrity or CEO moms talk about how they do it all because they're organized or because "somehow they just make it work," I want to scream. It's a lie—one that makes mega millionaires feel better about themselves but that makes the rest of us feel like we'll never measure up or that we must be doing something wrong. Here's the real truth: I get everything done because I have other people who help me do it all—when my kids are well *and* when they're sick as stink.

Your Partner

One year ago, my littlest came down with croup and spent 3 nights hacking away like a baby seal. I came home from work to her lying on the rug in my living room, curled up in a tiny ball, clutching a stuffed animal while my husband rubbed her back. Then, New Year's Day, she wound up in the emergency room after waking from a nap with a 103° F fever and labored, noisy breathing.

Needless to say, I had to force my mind to "think like a pediatrician" both of those evenings. I also had to take a deep breath and try *not* to think about all the work I would inevitably miss, the wasted child care dollars I would no doubt forfeit, and the sleepless nights I was bound to encounter before she recovered from her respiratory illness.

When your child is sick, it's inherently emotional. You may feel like only you can be there to watch over your little one, but remember to let your partner take the lead on bowing out of work or handling a sick day school pickup when it makes sense.

Family or Friends

You've got to build a network of people around you who can stand in for you when necessary. This is one of the most important reasons for developing at least a small tribe of other moms (or dads) or available family members who live in close proximity who you can count on.

How do you find a good tribe? When I sat down with perinatal mental health specialist Ann Marie Miner she put it like this: "Making adult friends is extremely difficult. It's way harder than it was when we were in preschool or kindergarten. Making adult friends requires forced vulnerability."

That's why infant mommy-and-me classes are so great at helping you bond with other parents. Almost all the participants are scared, unsure of how to raise their newborns. When caring for your baby doesn't go well or is confusing, you're in good company. You're also vulnerable enough at that moment to get help from others—even if you don't know them well—and that can eventually build meaningful relationships.

You can also develop vulnerable friendships through parallel learning activities like baby-and-me music classes and postnatal mama–baby or mama–tot exercise classes. I've developed some of my closest mom friendships over shared hikes and abdominal crunches. Now that my kids are a little older, I make it a point to chat at school pickup on my day off and to schedule playdates during times my daughters and I can attend. I've intentionally, slowly connected with other parents in my neighborhood. We may not end up as besties, but I know I can count on them if I need them.

Think Like a Pediatrician

As I remind myself to stay objective during my own kids' illnesses, all the sick kid parenting pearls I try to share with my patients' parents in clinic week after week are at the forefront of my mind.

Follow Your Gut

If you are worried about your child, call someone. Make an appointment. Get them in front of a pediatrician. You know your kid best, so if they seem off to you, listen to that little voice inside your head telling you to take action. Pediatricians aren't irritated when parents want their child to be seen "just to be sure everything is OK." Actually, we would much rather that than the alternative—a serious condition gone unchecked. Kids tend to rally well at first with sickness but then can crash pretty fast. It's better to get the parenting tips you need early on so you don't get to a more critical point.

If you're a new parent, that may mean you call your pediatrician as soon as your child develops a small cough. That is not a problem. Your child's doctor or nurse can listen to your questions and guide you through what to expect and what to do. Consider it your sick kid mini education. As you get more experienced, you'll gain confidence, you'll know the basic ways to handle minor illnesses, and you likely won't need as much assistance. But if you do, your pediatrician is always there for you.

You want to choose a doctor who is going to care for your child and is trained specifically in pediatrics. You want to feel comfortable with them and feel that you can ask all those questions that are on your mind. When you do have a choice, choose medical professionals with pediatric training so they can get the most accurate medical history possible and can provide the most up-to-date care.

Understand Honesty Is Important and Details Matter

If your child has had a fever for 1 day or for 10 days, those are completely different situations, each of which triggers different levels of testing and medical interventions, depending on your child's age. I've sat in clinics with my daughters just like you have, watching practitioners shrug a little when I tell them how bad they looked at home when I booked the appointment. In those moments, it's tempting to try to sell how bad the illness is. Sometimes, I know, it feels like elaborating a tiny bit to get the attention of health care professionals will help when it comes to a sick kid, but that can backfire. You don't want your child to have extra blood work, imaging (X-rays, etc), or medications when they don't need them. It can lead to unnecessary and sometimes harmful side effects and even hospitalizations.

Believe That We Believe You

I cannot count the number of times someone has brought their febrile child into my office, completely miserable, so that I can see how sick they really are. No fever reducers used, the poor kids and their well-intentioned parents must have had a horrible time on their car ride over to the clinic. But there's no need to show us your child at their worst. It's fine to give your son or daughter acetaminophen or ibuprofen before your doctor's visit (these medications can be age and condition dependent—check with your health professional if you're not sure). In fact, the best way for medical professionals to accurately assess how your child is doing can be to see them *without the fever* when possible, since they sometimes look worse than they actually are when febrile.

Using Antibiotics Judiciously

Sometimes, parents will seem disappointed when I tell them their child has an upper respiratory infection (aka a cold) and doesn't need antibiotics. Remember, it's a good thing if there isn't a need for extra medicine. You don't want antibiotics unless you really need them. Every drug has side effects, and if we give antibiotics for colds, the medication

• Doesn't change a thing about how fast a child gets better.

• May give them side effects like diarrhea or rashes.

• Contributes to antibiotic resistance (when an antibiotic stops working against the bacteria it was designed to treat and makes it harder and harder to treat serious illnesses).

It's hard to wait out a viral illness, letting the storm pass until the sun comes out again, but it's worth it to concentrate on comfort care if your doctor prescribes it versus fighting for an unnecessary medicine.

Accept Illnesses Can Change Quickly

When pediatricians see you in the office, we're catching your child at a moment in time. We hear about what has happened so far, and we base our diagnosis on our examination that day. It's one data point. Often, though, an illness can change within hours or days, and, without a crystal ball, it's impossible to predict which direction a sickness will go. It's not surprising to pediatricians when we need to schedule a recheck or follow-up appointment to make sure things are improved or when a parent calls us back to say a child is still sick. That's why we give so many contingency after-visit instructions. Most of the time, we can solve an issue with one evaluation, but it can take a bit more complex problem-solving with multiple visits at other times.

Find a Medical Professional Who Welcomes Your Questions
Part of my job as a pediatrician is to make sure I translate medical jargon for my patients and their parents, ensuring they leave with a solid understanding of what's wrong with their child and what they can expect as they recover. I know that it is sometimes terrifying (or sometimes just super inconvenient) to have a sick kid and that parents need answers and explanations. I'm used to it. All doctors are. So ask away. Clarify. Pull out the list of worries. Let us know the underlying issues (like, "When will my child be better, and when will I be able to go back to work?"). We're all ears, and, in the end, it's easier for all of us to be on the same page when you ask all of your questions from the get-go than to let frustration or confusion play a role in your child's illness.

Dealing with your kids' needs when they're sick is one of the most challenging parts of modern parenting, especially for working moms. The schedule rearranging, the miserable little one, the scary unknowns of illness—it all adds up. Remember, pediatricians know how hard it is to care for sick children (I do it myself all the time!), and we want your child to get better as fast as possible too. Access the resources you have, work on prevention first, make a care plan, and get the answers you need. Above all, follow your gut—if you're worried, get help.

Commuting

Being thoughtful about your commute is another way to minimize time away from your kids or to maximize your time alone. I used to hate commuting before I had my daughters. Of course, that was back when my biggest after-work decisions revolved around which happy hour chips-and-guacamole spot I was going to hit up with friends. Things change. So does perspective. My commute, like my showers, now offers some of my most tranquil moments, glimpses of my pre-child self, free and quiet.

I don't get much done in the shower, but the car is another situation altogether. It's where I listen to podcasts and audiobooks I've been meaning to catch up on. It's where I play hip-hop music *loud* on the way home from work. It's where I make audio notes to myself and hands-free calls to cross-country friends.

My commute is short, and that's the way I like it—20 minutes day-to-day and about 40 when I pitch in at our southern clinic location. My commute time is precious to me, but I don't want more of it. To me, time is money, and I don't want to waste either on shuffling myself and everyone I love from place to place, missing out on fresh air and downtime in the process.

Whenever possible, choose a short commute for yourself and for your kids' school. The car can be a great time for connecting with your family in an undistracted environment—I've had some of my best conversations with my daughter about the meaning of life on the way to gymnastics class—but, in general, the longer you have to drive, the more potential for hassle. Traffic, weather driving hazards, road rage—the less of those you have to deal with, the better.

"You really have to think about your time in terms of your hourly rate," says working mom Amanda, a mother of 2 who owns her own education consulting company. She chose her career, in part, because she wanted a more flexible schedule, whereas her husband works in a full-time office setting.

"When I think about cleaning my house, making extravagant meals, even driving a bunch of extra hours in the car, I'm always thinking about it like this: how much would I charge a client for all those extra minutes? My time is valuable. It's up to me how I want to spend it. I can't afford everything I want, but I can afford to prioritize what really matters to me. What I want the most is time."

I'm well aware that often commutes are nonnegotiable. If you're unhappy with how long your commute is, see if you can get creative with your hours. Take the early shift and get home before the worst traffic, or finish your day remotely from home. If you're paying for hourly child care, any time you spend in the car is time you're paying someone else to hang out with your child, so minimize it if you can.

Creating More Peace Within Your Home

Of all the things working moms I talk to regularly pine away for, it's a little peace when they get home. Working mom Leslie's house is anything but peaceful these days. The toys seem to multiply on the floor, despite her valiant attempts to keep them organized. The trash and recycling bins fill up with diapers and food scraps the moment she empties them. Her kids are at high volume and high intensity most of the time. In fact, she would call it mind-numbing. With twin preschoolers and a baby to take care of, she has her hands full.

The other night, Leslie's husband looked at her with weary eyes as they attempted to wrangle their boys at dinner. One was trying with all his might to stand on the table, the other whining bitterly about his vegetable options. "Why is it always like this with them?" her husband asked.

There are moments when Leslie is brought to tears by a question like that. At times she feels discouraged and tired of the constant mayhem her young boys bring to their lives. Leslie doesn't need to be perfect at being peaceful as she parents, but she'd like to be better at it.

I've learned a few parenting tips and tricks to stay peaceful and present when things get hectic (read: most days).

Peaceful Parenting Takes Intention

First and foremost, peaceful parenting doesn't happen by luck—it happens by intention. Sure, there are Zen master mamas out there who can't imagine being bothered by the sounds of multiple screaming children. Or worst, multiple screaming children screaming in unison. Those ladies are few and far between. That's definitely not me—if their tendency is toward calm, mine is toward mental overload. So, for all of us who weren't born relaxed, getting more responsive (versus reactive) to our babies or children takes a whole lot of effort and practice. Why? It's *easier* to get all riled up. It's what our bodies do naturally, as part of a fight-or-flight response to perceived danger.

The only problem is, when our infants wail or our toddlers flop themselves on the ground in protest, even though it's not usually an emergency or dangerous, our bodies can't tell we have a false alarm on our hands. Instead, our bodies do what they normally do when we sense danger—our heart rates go up, our blood pressures rise, we get hyperfocused and intense. Teaching ourselves to relax, to calm down, and to make conscious decisions about how we'll parent takes, sometimes, overriding our natural systems' tendencies.

It can take a while to learn how to do that. If you're a new parent (or even a parent-to-be already worked up about the whole kid thing), don't throw in the towel right away if it takes you weeks, or even months or years, to get the hang of it. Read about how to get mindful. Go to a guided meditation or yoga class where an expert can demonstrate how to get started. Practice, practice, practice. Forgive yourself when you mess up because you're, inevitably, going to.

Peaceful Parenting Takes Education

Peaceful parenting takes perspective and education. So many moms and dads I see in the clinic seem shocked as each developmental stage comes along. They are surprised by cluster feeding and colic, worried by stranger danger, and perplexed by toddler tantrums. It's understandable. There is so much to learn and know. My best advice? Read ahead! Get a baseline understanding of what's to come for your child developmentally from reputable sources. If you're still pregnant, invest in information about the newborn period and continue reading after your baby arrives.

Your baby or toddler may not have all the same challenges as her peers, but she's bound to have at least some of them! The more you know, the more you will feel empowered and ready to face those "why are they like this all the time?" moments with confidence.

Peaceful Parenting Takes Self-care

Second—and you already know this if you've read this far—peaceful parenting takes self-care. There is absolutely no way for parents—new or experienced—to parent peacefully without taking care of themselves on a regular basis. Our kids notice when we're stressed—they feel it, their little neurons pick up on it. They also notice when we're content, balanced, and relaxed. Yep, there is no faking it when it comes to setting a good example for our children. Self-care takes time, commitment, and a realization that, in the end, we'll have a lot more family joy if we first find joy ourselves.

Peaceful Parenting Takes Partnership

Finally, peaceful parenting takes partnership. I don't only mean co-parent partnership, though having another adult in your house obviously means more hands around to get things done. I mean community. Motherhood was never meant to be attempted in a box, by ourselves, without the help of, literally, a village. But we try too often to muscle through it alone, ignoring the input or the assistance of others. Or we rely on superficial social media connections. The truth is, if you're going to be a peaceful parent, it's going to take community—live friends, family, or a partner (or all 3!)—sharing the hardships and the celebrations of raising small children in real, face-to-face interactions.

✂❀✂❀✂❀

The chaos in Leslie's house won't be changing anytime soon, just like it won't be changing anytime soon in my own home. When someone asks me how my girls are, I tend to say, "Well, it was touch and go there last week, but today we're all hanging in there." Because it's true. And real. And, it's also true that in the middle of the drama I awake to so often, there's peace—not around me, but inside. Or at least I'm moving in that direction because I know that I am my kids' greatest teacher. If they see stress, they will learn stress. If they see love, perspective, and collaboration, they will learn those important lessons too.

Caring for the Needs of All Our Children

If you have more than 1 child, balancing all of their practical needs can be a challenge. Thank goodness my second daughter was born in the same season as my first so I could reuse most of the clothes I bought the first time around 3 years later. Even more challenging, though, is caring for their emotional needs—making sure they all feel loved and care for.

My love for my 2 girls is different—not more or less—just different. They have their own temperaments and their own love languages. One of them needs tickles and laughter and is loud most of the time. The other needs quiet and security and coziness. They have their own preferences. One loves everything ballet and pink. The other loves soccer balls and dirt. Most importantly, they have their own parenting needs.

One is rowdy and bullheaded. The other is opinionated but anxious.

A lot of parents I meet worry about how they'll love or parent their kids equally when their second baby arrives. They worry about how they'll extend the same level of energy they gave their first child to another boy or girl. They wonder if they have it in them—if they could ever love another human being so intensely.

Working mom Monica, a mom of 2, told me how she made room in her heart when she had her second child.

> I remember the day I brought Lilly home from the hospital. Her big brother Jack was looking over at her, and he made some gesture toward her. It was a sudden move with his arm and, in my sleepless state, I thought that he might injure her, that for whatever reason he might hit her or that he was being aggressive towards her. It was a split-moment feeling that I had, probably due to high levels of postpartum hormones and low levels of emotional reserves, and definitely not based in reality. I felt myself instinctively protecting my baby, jerking her away from my son, crouching over her so that he couldn't get to her. And, I also got, for one split moment, really angry at him. The mama bear in me came out that day. I'd had that protective feeling billions of times for him throughout his short life—when another child said something unkind at school, when he injured himself playing at the park—but I hadn't thought it was possible until that incident to protect another person like that. That was the moment that I realized I could love 2 people with the same level of raw intensity at once.

I learned exactly what Monica meant with my own kids when that protective feeling kicked in for my second child postpartum in some maternal instinct moment. I've been over the moon for her ever since. Still, as she grows up and becomes more and more human, it's tempting to see second-time parenting as an exercise in missed documentation and attention. It's the same for all multikid families. We're busy once we have 2, and we feel worried that our second (or third or fourth) child will, eventually, feel slighted by us. It's hard to not constantly compare what we're doing for one child versus the other. We could try to give exactly the same level of attention and time, to ensure that everything is fair. But, if we are constantly aiming to make everything we do with or for our kids perfectly equal, we miss out on the things that make them feel sincerely valued and cared for. We also end up pretty tired from all that math.

Instead, focus on taking advantage of opportunities to be with each of your children individually as they arise, even if they arise spontaneously. Look for ways to invest in them on the basis of the ways they need it. Maybe one needs a special trip away—just the 2 of you. Maybe the other needs you to coach his baseball team. Aim for balance over weeks and months. There will be stretches of time when 1 child may need you more, and that's OK. When the dust settles, think about ways to even things out. Give love and attention according to the ways they, as individuals, receive love and attention best.

You may feel, like I do sometimes, like loving your kids well means loving them in perfect measure, but I challenge that notion. Obviously, don't play favorites, don't be neglectful, but do focus less on loving equally, more on loving specifically, fully, with presence. Celebrate how you're stronger, wiser, and, yeah, a bit less microfocused. Your kids don't need your equality as much as they need your individualized, real, uncalculated love.

Our kids matter. Their feelings matter. Their sense of connection to us matters. Prioritizing them matters. When we're at our wisest, we're clearly able to see that; when we become mothers, our kids are not an addition to our lives, they *are* our lives. Caring for and carving out time for the people we love most is about setting aside moments to be together, looking for our kids' deeper needs, and approaching motherhood for all our children as less of a perfect balancing act and more of an intentional practice.

Chapter 9

What's for Dinner?

You don't have to cook fancy or complicated masterpieces—
just good food from fresh ingredients.
— Julia Child

*E*very Monday through Friday evening after work, working mom Marissa has a set routine. She clocks out at 6:00
pm from her job as a teller at the local credit union, walks to
her car, and calls her kids. And almost every Monday through
Friday, like clockwork, they ask her the exact same thing:
"What's for dinner?"

Sometimes Marissa's prepared with a quick answer or
idea. "There are leftovers on the top shelf," or "Check the
cupboard for spaghetti—do we still have some left?" Most
nights, though, she finds herself creating a plan on the spot.

> I don't mean to be so last-minute about it, it's just, my
> kids may have food on the brain all day every day, but
> I sure don't. From the minute I arrive at the office to
> the minute I leave, I'm thinking about providing good
> customer service and accurately counting out bills. The
> last thing that pops into my mind is how to get a hot
> meal on the table in the middle of all that...until about
> 6:05 when the kids remind me, that is.

Marissa's in good company. Although we all want to
consistently feed our kids nutritious meals in a way that
promotes a healthy relationship with food and creates times
for positive family interactions, actually *doing it* is quite

another feat for busy working moms. Answering the question "What's for dinner?" doesn't have to be so daunting, though, especially when you focus on savvy meal planning, efficient preparation, and family mealtime enjoyment.

Savvy Meal Planning

Keep Midweek Meals Simple

First things first: let yourself off the hook. You are not a full-time home chef. You are a working woman, and your time is more limited than it is for other moms. Don't feel bad if you can't provide a freshly cooked meal every night from scratch. Sometimes calling the whole thing off and ordering cheap takeout is the way to take care of your family holistically—both your mental and your physical health. If you do order out, choose the healthiest options possible whenever possible, knowing that sometimes, even that can be too much on a particularly hard day.

When you do cook, choose some go-to meals you know will be quick and easy for the nights you work and meal preparation seems most exhausting. At my house, it's chicken and broccoli Mondays, grilled fish taco Tuesdays, and stir-fry Wednesdays. To make my life even easier, I buy high-quality meat in bulk and freeze it. The night before I need it, I put what I need for the next night in the refrigerator to thaw so I can add grains, vegetables, and side dishes easily when I come home from work.

Working mom Liselle works part time as a newborn photographer. She meets clients at odd hours—before and after work or on the weekends—so that she's available for school drop-off and pickup for her twin third graders. She tries to keep the fridge stocked with healthy snacks, but putting together a complete meal while the boys ask for homework assistance and she edits photos or tries to juggle client appointments feels overwhelming, especially on days they

Snack Ideas for Families: Foods to Keep on Hand

Type	Suggestions
Fresh Fruit	• Apples, bananas, peaches, nectarines, pears • Cherries, grapes, plums (sliced or pitted) • Orange or grapefruit sections • Strawberries, grapes (cut into half for small children)
Dried Fruit	• Apples, apricots, peaches, pears (cut up) • Dates, prunes • Raisins, cranberries
Vegetables	• Carrot sticks, celery sticks • Raw or steamed cauliflower, broccoli • Bell pepper strips—red, yellow, orange, and green • Grape and cherry tomatoes • Fresh or frozen corn and peas • Sliced cucumbers • Avocado slices or chunks
Lean Protein	• Fish (canned tuna, salmon, sardines, whitefish) • Peanut butter or other nut butters (smoot, spread on whole grain bread or crackers) • Edamame beans or chickpeas or hummus spreads • Cooked tofu cubes or tofu dip • Hard boiled eggs
Dairy Products	• Cheese (sliced, grated, or diced) • Cottage cheese • Low-sugar yogurt • Milk—cow's milk or non-dairy milks
Breads & Cereals	• Whole wheat bread • Whole grain tortillas or tortilla chips • Whole grain crackers • Whole grain dry cereals • Rice cakes • Whole grain pitas and bagels • Air-popped popcorn

From American Academy of Pediatrics. Choosing healthy snacks for kids. HealthyChildren. org. Updated January 31, 2020. Accessed November 16, 2020. https://www.healthychildren. org/English/healthy-living/nutrition/Pages/Choosing-Healthy-Snacks-for-Children.aspx have soccer practice. She's learned to keep it simple midweek. "I have my weekday standards," she says. "They're not fancy, but they work."

Use the Weekends for More Extensive Cooking

On weekends, when you have more mental bandwidth to enjoy experimenting with new recipes, that's your chance to refine your culinary prowess, if that's your thing. Consider using more relaxed times to create family memories around meals as well, like Saturday morning pancakes and eggs or Friday night backyard cookouts. Use family mealtimes to instill a sense of comradery and to develop a routine of household chores. Elementary school–aged children can help with clearing and setting the table, washing dishes, and running the dishwasher.

Spend time on more extensive meal preparation and planning Saturdays or Sundays, and make large double batches of 2 separate meals that can easily be reheated later. Eat half of the first meal Sunday evening, then half of the second meal Monday. On Tuesday and Wednesday, eat the leftovers. You'll get 4 days' worth of dinner for only 1 day of effort. Working mom Pilar, a seasoned mom of 4, told me when her kids were little she started cooking this way and still does when the oldest is home from college break!

Shop Online

Consider online grocery shopping as a way to build efficiency and to spend less overall on your food budget. Sometimes when you're at the grocery store in person, that shopping cart fills up pretty quickly, especially when you have kids in tow who just *need* that extra box of cereal. Grocery shopping when you are hungry is never a good idea, as you always tend to put more items in your cart than you really need. I've been surprised by my total at the checkout more than a few times, but it can be embarrassing or just inconvenient to return what I've selected to the checker.

Online grocery shopping can give you more control financially. As you fill your cart virtually, it's easy to see your running total and to adjust if you need to before you submit your payment. Online shopping also allows you to shop from multiple stores efficiently. Use big-box grocery stores for pantry and refrigerator staples, and purchase specialty or harder-to-find items from local markets or traditional grocers.

"I live and die by Instacart and Amazon Prime," working mom Sylvia told me in the clinic a few weeks ago. She has 3 kids—a 7-year-old, a 9-year-old, and a 12-year-old—and works part time as a hair stylist. "I don't how moms managed before online shopping existed."

Avoid Prepackaged Meals

Avoid fully prepackaged meals when possible. Many have high sodium content (which you want to stay away from) and can taste bad once in the freezer for extended periods of time. Often you can make the same types of meals just as easily by purchasing separate packages of frozen veggies and meat, then adding your own sauce for less sodium overall.

Resist purchasing large quantities of sugary snacks too, so they're not as readily available to you or your family when hunger strikes and cravings kick in. When my youngest daughter turned 3 and developed a penchant for sneaking the marshmallows we purchased for summer camping trips from our pantry, we decided to get rid of them altogether. Same went for candy, ice cream, and salty chips. When we do buy them now for special occasions, it's more intentional and enjoyable.

Creating a Healthy Relationship With Food for Your Family

Babies Ready to Start Solid Foods

Offer as Many Varied Foods as Possible From an Early Age
The American Academy of Pediatrics recommends starting solid foods at about 6 months of age. They also recommend waiting 2 to 3 days between new foods to observe your infant for any allergic reactions. But, starting at about 6 months, there are no limitations on what these foods can be (except no honey and no cups of cow's milk until 1 year of age). There are no "adult" flavors and "baby" flavors, just kid and baby consistencies. Why not offer pureed mushrooms, eggplant, artichokes, kale, or yams? In fact, the American Academy of Allergy, Asthma, and Immunology now recommends even highly allergenic foods like shellfish, dairy, peanut butter or peanut-containing snacks, and eggs be introduced earlier versus later. We know that food preferences start even within the womb and that giving our children a wide variety of flavors and textures early on promotes a diverse palate and healthier lifelong nutrition.

Don't Give Up Too Soon
An expression of disgust does not predict a life of hatred. It can take multiple exposures before babies develop an affinity for a new flavor. Working mom Jamie's daughter's first food was avocado. She has pictures of Remy's sweet little face just covered in it at 6 months, with a look of utter displeasure. She spat that food out as fast as Jamie could get it to her lips. Of course, Jamie didn't force it on her that day, but every week she reintroduced a small amount as part of the other foods she offered. With Remy at 1 year of age, Jamie took another picture of Remy's face covered in a green gooey mess, this time with a look of complete glee. Avocado became and still is her favorite food to eat.

Toddlers

Model Good Behavior

Your kids are listening to what you say, noticing how you treat other people, and, yes, watching what you eat. That means that if you want them to eat more healthily, you might need to adjust what food is on your plate. It won't work to have you order a cheeseburger and a soda every time you go out as a family if you want your kids to eventually do the opposite. (See "Tips and Tricks for Restaurant Success With Kids in Tow" box later in this chapter.) You may need to take stock of what you yourself are consuming. If you eat healthy, high-quality foods, it allows your children to see healthy, high-quality foods as normal.

Remind Yourself of the Responsibilities You and Your Child Each Bring to the Table

As a parent, your responsibility is to provide healthy options for your child at consistent intervals during the day. The child's responsibility is to choose how much of any given food to eat at any given time. Offer healthy options, and let your child choose what he or she wants to consume from those offerings. If your child decides he or she doesn't want the green beans tonight? That's OK. Just don't offer a replacement food when she won't eat them, and definitely don't use those beans as a reward for dessert.

Remember That Most Kids Go Through Phases When They're More Picky About What They Eat or Less Interested in Food Overall

Sometimes in a toddler's mind, green equals poisonous plant (or just equals new thing I've never tried before), which equals bad. Instead of creating power struggles at one isolated meal, instead take the long view: raising individuals who savor what they consume, who use it as fuel to drive their lives, and who have the freedom to enjoy it fully.

Grade School and Older Children

Follow these recommendations from the American Academy of Pediatrics for grade school children to make sure your children get the nutrients they need throughout the week.

Making Healthy Food Choices

These five groups and typical minimum servings are:

Vegetables: 3–5 servings per day. A serving may consist of 1 cup of raw leafy vegetables, ¾ cup of vegetable juice, or ½ cup of other vegetables, chopped raw or cooked.

Fruits: 2–4 servings per day. A serving may consist of ½ cup of sliced fruit, ¾ cup of fruit juice, or a medium-size whole fruit, like an apple, banana, or pear.

Bread, cereal, or pasta: 6–11 servings per day. Each serving should equal 1 slice of bread, ½ cup of rice or pasta, or 1 ounce of cereal.

Protein foods: 2–3 servings of 2–3 ounces of cooked lean meat, poultry, or fish per day. A serving in this group may also consist of ½ cup of cooked dry beans, one egg, or 2 tablespoons of peanut butter for each ounce of lean meat.

Dairy products: 2–3 servings per day of 1 cup of low-fat milk or yogurt, or 1½ ounces of natural cheese.

From the American Academy of Pediatrics. Making healthy food choices. HealthyChildren. org. Updated May 28, 2020. Accessed November 16, 2020. https://www.healthychildren.org/ English/ages-stages/gradeschool/nutrition/Pages/Making-Healthy-Food-Choices.aspx

Encourage Your Children Whenever Possible to Help You With Making Meal Plans and Preparations

Go to the library or look online with your kids to find recipe collections they're excited about. Pick a favorite cookbook or family-friendly cooking website and work your way through it together to avoid ruts. Use lazier days when you're not working and they don't have extracurricular activities planned to spend time mixing and mincing in the kitchen. Allowing young kids to contribute to family food preparation contributes to healthier eating overall. (For more information, see "Tips and Tricks to Involve Young Kids in Family Meal Preparation" box later in this chapter.) Your kids will be more willing to try foods that they helped prepared.

Give Older Kids the Responsibility of Planning, Purchasing, and Preparing a Full Meal for the Entire Family Once a Week as an Opportunity to Contribute

Give them parameters for including a variety of food groups. Have them join you to add all the ingredients they need to your virtual shopping cart, or bring them with you to the grocery store. Then, have them choose a new recipe for the next week.

Grow a Garden, Even if It's a Mini One

Kids who help grow and make their food have a more rich experience with source ingredients and are often less picky. Even 3-year-olds can help you garden. Let them taste test the mint or cherry tomatoes directly from your backyard plants after you wash them. They can even help you decide what seeds to buy early in the season, creating even more buy-in. If you don't have an outdoor space or room for a garden, consider a windowsill herb garden. Take your kids to farmers markets to expose your children to where their food is coming from.

Working mom Carla told me, "I can remember the first time Jaun saw all the produce. He just loved trying all the fruit and vegetable samples and talking to the vendors. We made going to the farmers market a Saturday morning tradition starting at 1 year old."

Tips and Tricks to Involve Young Kids in Family Meal Preparation

Delegate According to Age and Skill Level

- Older kids might like setting the table or creating a beautiful fruit platter.
- Younger kids can measure out portions and help with mixing.
- Involve kids in chopping and peeling with age-appropriate kid knives and child-sized whisks and spoons.

Give Your Kids Choices and Responsibility

- Let your kids look through recipe books to choose side dishes or sauces on their own.
- Expect some mess, but also expect some help cleaning up the kitchen.

Allow Experimentation

- Letting kids add in a few extra ingredients to your planned recipe can literally spice things up for kids, allowing them to flex their science and culinary muscles.

Stay Away From Repetition

- Switch things up each time you cook. If one child always empties the dishwasher or always uses the mixer, food preparation will be less interesting and kids won't have the advantage of learning multiple skills.

Eating Healthy on the Go

Plan ahead for food needs on the fly. Research your healthiest options ahead of time so when your crew is hungry, you have an idea of where to head. (See "Tips and Tricks—Choosing Healthy Fast-Food Options" box later in this chapter.) Many fast-food or national café chains offer healthier options like

Tips and Tricks—Choosing Healthy Fast-Food Options

You Should

- Choose smaller portion sizes.
- Ask for nutritional information.
- Special order if needed to make meals healthier.
- Skip the unhealthy sides like french fries or chips.

You Should NOT

- Assume salads or other healthy-sounding foods are your best option.
- Add on a high-calorie beverage like fruit juice or soda.

Choose Foods That Are

- High in fiber
- Whole grain
- Grilled or roasted
- Fresh fruits and vegetables

Avoid Foods That Are

- Fried or covered in cream sauce
- High in saturated fats
- High in sodium

Tips and Tricks for Restaurant Success With Kids in Tow

Choose Your Restaurant Wisely
Pay attention to your child's mood, sleep level, and, generally, how things are going that day when you pick your place to eat.

Avoid the Kid Menu
Skip the chicken strips and fries. Instead, order sides of healthier foods off the adult menu or offer the food on your plate to your kids.

Plan Your Escape Route
As soon as the food comes and you've gotten all the extra sauces and utensils you need, ask your server to bring the check so that if things devolve you can leave quickly.

Bring Your Own (Multiple Distractions)
Pack lightweight, screen-free distraction options like coloring books and crayons and thin paperback books each time you head out to eat with your little ones.

grilled chicken sandwiches, protein packs with eggs and cheese, or fresh sliced fruit or veggies.

Working mom Monique struggled with finding inexpensive ways to feed her son and daughter healthily without relying on fast food when she became a parent. When she was growing up, her parents relied on drive-through meals most mornings on the way to school. "I try to make home-cooked meals as much as possible, but the convenience of a drive-through is always there, since I'm usually not even thinking about dinner until I leave my job at my company's fulfillment center every day. Now, when I do go to fast food,

I try my best to think about avoiding fried options and looking for fruits and vegetables or for proteins with less fat."

Always remember to prepack a lunch box with a cooler pack in it to store items like precut cucumber slices or carrots, cubed cheese, lean meat, or yogurts from your own fridge when you're on the go for after-school activities with older kids or child care or preschool pickup with little ones. "I always offer a fresh snack first," says working mom Lauren, a mom of 3, "but I keep backup prepackaged snacks like whole grain crackers or roasted nuts with me in my purse and glove compartment in case we whip through our main stash. It's better than having to stop with my teenagers on the fly."

Make Mealtimes Enjoyable, Not Perfect

There are no place mats, and we only have paper towels for napkins. The dinner tonight? A take-and-bake barbecue chicken pizza and (because I'm a pediatrician) a large salad. It's not even close to the healthiest meal we'll have this year. We just moved back to our home after having lived at my parents', and we're celebrating. There are boxes piled high in the dining room, and we're all covered in grime from unpacking and sorting all day. My arms are sore from rearranging furniture. Each time I lift them, they tell me how unhappy they are. But we're happy because we're here at last, sharing a meal together, laughing, and talking about what we're most excited to reexplore in our own neighborhood. "Michael's coffee shop!" the little one squeals. "No! That climbing structure at the playground! Mom, can we go there tomorrow? Please?"

My husband and I exchange grateful glances. Gosh, it feels good to sit here and eat this food together. Sometimes the most important part of what's for dinner is what is actually for dinner—the food you consume and the love you put into creating it as a family. Sometimes it's about teaching

family responsibilities, and "can I be excused" before getting up, and "tell me about the good and bad of your day."
Sometimes, though, what's for dinner is about the mood
you set, the way you catch the cheese as it drips down your
daughter's chin, the giggles as your baby crawls into your
arms, the pure enjoyment of being a family.

Not every meal you make will be perfectly nutritious.
Some weeks you'll barely be able to get food on the table,
much less make sure its components are well-rounded. In
seasons, you may get in a rut, stuck preparing the same
foods again and again. You will most definitely pick the least
healthy item on the menu at the drive-through from time
to time and bring no snacks in the car when you need them
most. That's OK. Your goal as a working mom is to do the
best you can when you can—in all areas of motherhood, but
especially in this one—and to use efficiency tricks and pre-
planning regimens as the tools they are, not as extra stressors. Sure, what's for dinner is sometimes just about getting
food on the table, but it can be about more than that if we
don't get caught up in doing it perfectly. If we have the right
perspective, it can be about joy—coming together with the
people we love most to unwind, to celebrate, or simply just
to be.

Chapter 10

Allow and Expect Others to Be Equal Partners in Parenting

Women will have achieved true equality when men share with them the responsibility of bringing up the next generation.

— *Ruth Bader Ginsburg*

Lindsay and Chad always talked about the kind of parents they would be: equal partners, the kind of people who cared for each other and for their children as teammates. Lindsay studied marketing and worked for an up-and-coming firm downtown. Chad was rising through the ranks at a biotech job he landed right out of his master's program. They were both college-educated, progressive professionals who valued each other's contributions at work and at home. Somewhere along the line, though, their plan dissolved after their son James came along. It wasn't intentional, but it was disappointing, especially for Lindsay.

> Working mom Lindsay was in my office at their son's 9-month well-child check. "Chad loves James and me—that much is clear. We share a lot of parenting responsibilities. Obviously, we are beyond some kind of *Mad Men* existence, but, when it comes down to it, I am the one with all the family life burden. I arrange our child care. I make sure we have all the baby gear we

need. Here I am at the doctor's today, rushing in from
an important work meeting. It really makes me want to
keep score so I can show him how much more work I am
putting in—at both my day job and at my parenting job."

If you're a working mom with a working male co-parent,
I'm sure you understand just what she's saying. On the
whole, same-sex partnerships seem to avoid the same pitfalls of gender-role expectations when running a household.
If I asked you to keep a tally of who does more—you or
your partner—to make your family run, I know you would
be like, "Please bring it on. I'm going to win every time." I
mean, that's incredibly true in my own home—one where
my husband and I both work, where I'm the breadwinner,
where I consider myself a very liberated, modern mom. I realize there are all types of family structures, and I know some
advanced, enlightened families where this is not the case, but,
for the vast majority of women out there, this is the reality.
Think about the laundry detergent ordering, the sleep training, the lunch making, the playdate arranging that you do. If
you really did keep score, it would be a total shutout.

Just last week, I got so over-the-top mad as I tried to
co-parent, I swear steam started coming out of my ears. My
husband was not doing what I needed him (wanted him) to
do fast enough, the way I'd do it, or with the same level of
intensity I thought it required. He was putting it off, waiting
until the last minute, choosing to watch a show on the couch
with his feet up and his craft beer in hand instead of jumping
into action. We had a lot to get done before Monday hit, and
my mental check list load was piling up while his seemed to
be shrinking.

What was so pressing? Making a 5-year-old's lunch. Yeah,
I was all worked up over packing turkey and cheese into a
hot pink lunch box for my daughter's school day. I'd asked
him to do it about an hour before, and there was still a loaf

of cheddar on the counter with no other signs of progress in sight. It was irking me to no end.

It's not the first time I've gotten all up in arms over something completely insignificant, and it's not the first time we've had tension over shared responsibilities and division of labor. A seasoned marriage, 2 kids, 2 (plus) careers, and a 30-year mortgage puts pressure on even the best-intentioned partners. And, as my husband and I sort out how to balance our own individual needs and desires with the needs of our family, there's often some dissonance. The more I talk to other moms—especially working moms like me—the more I find a common struggle to be a modern mom in relationships that are still in the process of becoming modern.

Here's what I mean: my husband and I both work full time. I plan the meals, buy the clothes, do the laundry, sign my kids up for all the activities, make sure the school projects are completed. My husband does *a lot* (far more than making simple lunches), but when it comes to our house, our lives, and our kids, I take on the mental load.

I'm not whining, I'm just stating facts. The June 25, 2020, news release from the Bureau of Labor Statistics stated that women still do more unpaid household tasks in most households, even if they're primary breadwinners like I am. Turns out gender norms may be changing in the workplace relatively rapidly, but, on the home front, things are often still a little archaic.

My partner is a caring guy who wants the best for our family and who values equality and teamwork. He's all for both of us pursuing our passions and working together to support our kids, but he and I still somehow struggle, no matter how modern we've tried to make our marriage.

I mean, just a generation or 2 ago, our lives as working moms would have seemed ludicrous to most. Our parents and their parents all divided tasks, generally, along gender lines. That wasn't always fair, and it definitely left women without opportunities and options, but, when it came to relationships, it probably was at least less confusing. You do this (child care, housework, home life), and I'll do that (work at a job outside of the home).

You still see vestiges of the old mentality whenever multiple generations gather for holidays or in social settings. Almost every month in my office, some sweet grandma will come along to the first newborn checkup, smiling at her son as he changes his baby girl's diaper with swagger.

"He's such a good father, isn't he?" she asks me.

If by that she means he is able to perform some basic tasks related to keeping a child from getting a urinary tract infection, then *yes*, for sure. And, when I see the dads beaming from the praise, I just smile back and nod. But, the reality is, helping with a few diaper changes isn't going to cut it for the "Dad of the Year" award anymore. Most moms I know expect more than that in this day and age.

I'm not complaining about modern-day dads. I'm also not saying all family structures or family struggles are the same — far from it — or that all dads are even the same. In fact, I feel kind of bad for modern dads. I mean, not as bad as I feel for modern-day moms. But I do feel bad. It seems like, when we empowered women to be just as fierce in the workplace as at home, forever changing modern-day motherhood, we forgot about educating men on how to change their perspectives on modern-day fatherhood.

We figured they would just adjust without any effort or preparation, magically skilled and knowledgeable in all things baby or toddler. We wrote them hardly any books and developed hardly any support groups or resources for them on the topic. Add in the Mr Mom monikers and the media depictions of helpless new dads fumbling through parenting — it's a not a surprise a lot of dads I see aren't sure exactly where they fit into the new parenting paradigm. By the way, before you send me a note describing how your partner is the bomb and has it all together and doesn't need books or resources, please realize I meet tons of amazingly talented fathers every day who are just amazing in the modern dad department—I know not all dads' struggles are alike, just like not all moms' struggles are alike.

Successful Working Moms

How do successful working moms share the responsibilities and pressures of work and home with their partners in a way that approaches equality and true partnership?

I sat down and talked with other working moms about how they successfully handle home and life balance with their significant others. Some work from home, some are high-level executives, but they all used these common tactics to work as a team.

They Don't Aim for an Even Fifty-Fifty Split

Working mom Lorinda knows that some areas of her partnership will not be evenly divided. Laundry may be 90% in her bucket, but cooking may only be 10%. She may do 30% of the accounting and bill paying, but her partner does 70% of the school pickups and drop-offs. She's most intentional about making sure she's not taking on 70% of *everything*, tipping the scales toward herself for every to-do that keeps their lives running.

They Make Their Partners Aware of the Tasks They're Carrying and of When They're Feeling Overwhelmed: They Share Their Mental Load

Working mom Mary, a couple's therapist, explained that, instead of telling her husband what to do, *she* spends a lot of time just sitting down with her spouse listing off what *she* needs to get done (or make decisions about) and then asking her husband to do the same. She comes at it from the perspective that there are a lot of times she knows her husband has no idea about all the things she's trying to manage and that there must be some things he's thinking about that she has no idea about too. She's giving him the benefit of the doubt. How does she get the conversation started? They plan what she calls family business meetings; put them on the calendar ("I'd love to say every week, but, let's be real, we have 2 young kids"); and, just like they map out their finances, they talk through their responsibilities.

They Divide Based on Strengths and Weaknesses — or Based on Practical Time or Financial Considerations

Working mom Gina, a self-employed businesswoman, explained: "Hey, I've got a job where, if I don't go to work, we potentially lose out on thousands of billable dollars."

If that mom doesn't work for a day, no one brings in money for her small business. Her husband, on the other hand, works for a traditional organization that offers paid sick days and vacation days as part of his compensation package. If he misses a day of work, it's stressful, but it's not earth-shattering. Although the world may still expect her to drop everything to pick up her child at child care for an illness, that just doesn't make sense for them.

"That doesn't mean that, sometimes, my desire to be with my kids when there's a problem doesn't win out over left-brain analytics and money, but 9 times out of 10, the choice is a no-brainer."

If you're a new mom and you're breastfeeding, this is an even simpler delineation point. For the duration of your breastfeeding experience, you are the "feeder in chief." Your partner should be the "soother in chief." Let your partner have the responsibility of getting educated on the best soothing techniques out there and make him the go-to person when the baby is cranky. If you are not a new parent, figure out some other "in chief" responsibilities you can divide.

My husband is also the "nail cutter in chief" and the "get the kids ready for bed in chief."

They Use a Common Language When Talking About What Needs to Get Done

Working mom Helen, a mom who works part time, explained that, since her partner is a businessman, she uses business team lingo when trying to divide and conquer.

"So, I'm trying to strategize about how we'll get everything accomplished for Leah's start to the school year. Let's talk through the components we need to make this successful."

Working mom Carol described her approach based on her and her husband's mutual love of sports.

"Listen, what part of the team can you head up the next few weeks? If we're going to win with everything going on this month, we're really going to have to work hard."

They Use Technology to Their Advantage, Including Shared Calendars, Communication Apps, and Online Shareable Corkboards, Trip Planners, and Lists

Of course, sometimes it's better just to go low-tech when you really want to accomplish something. I still make lists in a paper notebook and affix magnetic whiteboards and paper meal planners to my fridge.

In the End, They Choose to Ignore and Realize That, Sometimes, They Are Just Not Going to Be Happy

They, just like me, totally ignore eye rolls, small huffs, and pained expressions when it comes to handing off a little more of their mental loads to their partners.

"I feel like I just have to get over it when I perceive that my husband is annoyed when I let him know what he needs to do so we can keep our house and our home running," said one mom. "I get it. No one wants to be told what to do, but, in the process of off-loading some of my mental load, sometimes that's just how it has to happen."

They Extend Grace to Themselves and to Their Partners as We All Make This Pretty Complicated Transition

"Sometimes you don't get all the recognition you feel like you deserve (when you're a mom)," another working mom told me. "Sometimes I feel like my husband should be on the sidelines with the biggest, loudest megaphone, painted sign, pom-poms, shirt with my name on it, screaming at the top of his lungs about how amazing I'm doing at life...and when I look over and his eyes are closed on the couch, I first think what the heck? And secondly I think, am I doing that for him? (That's when I realize) he's doing 'it all' too."

They Take a Giant Step Back

It's annoying to have someone looking over your shoulder, micromanaging your every move. If you've ever had a super-controlling boss or even a nitpicky parent, you know the feeling. When someone doesn't trust us or tries to manage us, it makes us feel resentful and irritated. We sometimes even lose our organic interest in the topic and stop putting our best effort into it.

That's just what happens when we don't allow our partners to play an equal role in taking care of our children. We kind of sabotage our hope of true co-parenting. Instead, be conscious about how to empower your other half to be the parenting boss more often. That might mean actually leaving the house so he or she has the space to parent without your eagle eyes. It definitely will mean holding your tongue (or your own sighs or eye rolls or judgment) if he or she is not doing things exactly how you would do it.

Real Mom Reality Check

I am being honest with you—I don't do this perfectly in my own home all the time. You're reading this for some honesty, and that's what I'm going to give you.

My partner and I, we're still figuring things out in this area. Sometimes I feel like my husband thinks he's "babysitting" or "helping me out" instead of co-parenting. Sometimes he says he feels like I can't let go of being the family boss. If he had more freedom and less criticism when it came to his parenting decisions, he would feel more ownership and would be more motivated to step up in his co-team leader role. (For more information see the "The Principles Successful Moms (Try Their Best to) Co-parent By" box later in this chapter.)

Despite centuries—no, millennia—of societal norms, we continue to strive toward the idea that gender should make no difference when it comes to caring for our kids (kind of like how it didn't make a difference when I promoted him to soother in chief during the newborn period).

We are the first generation of moms who are trying to and are expected to "do it all." We're forging a new path as we parent and as we partner. It's a path where gender roles

The Principles Successful Moms (Try Their Best to) Co-parent By

- Letting each other parent as much as possible without co-parent oversight (as long as the other person is not doing something obviously detrimental or potentially abusive—there is a time and a place for stepping in)
- Setting expectations that we'll each get some time to ourselves throughout the week while the other person takes on a caregiver-in-chief role
- Paying attention to how we're both doing in terms of rest and stress
- Stepping in when we can tell the other person is overwhelmed or overworked

don't necessarily define tasks and responsibilities, *strengths* do—one where things aren't always even or completely balanced—for our kids or for ourselves.

Maximizing Time With Your Partner so You Have a Strong Foundation

We also take time to be with one another. When I tell other moms I'm going away with my partner for a romantic weekend, they often seem shocked. Like, "You're going to leave your kids—not for 1 night, but for *2 or 3 whole nights?!*" Yes, yes, I am. In the same way that I know that taking care of myself physically and mentally is important for my kids, I also know that taking care of my relationship with my partner is vital to our success as co-parents. The payout is 1,000-fold when we take trips, get out of our to-do lists, and get back to the things that made us fall in love in the first place. It does not have to be sensational or over the top. It just needs to be intentional.

Getaways

My husband and I love traveling together. Whenever we talk about our priorities and our vision for the future, it most always includes some discussion about owning a home on the ocean or traveling around the world. I remember, back before we had our first daughter and we faced our new parenthood reality, people telling us that we should take advantage of the time because, once she was around, all the trips we were taking would not be a possibility.

Fast-forward to our lives now. Most of the special time we spend together is made up of quick dates, moments it seems we have to steal away from our children if we want them to happen at all. We go out for 2 or 3 hours, leaving them with a sitter or with their grandparents. Our time together, just like the individual time we have to take care of ourselves, is most often dispersed as microdeposits to our relationship bank account. Every once in a while, though, that's not quite enough. We need a few completely free days, with no schedule and with no end point—days when we are in the presence of each other but we have no demands on each other, to deeply connect again.

I have taken vacations away with my husband because, honestly, I don't think we would survive without them. From time to time we need a macro getaway. Once in a blue moon, those vacations are over-the-top fancy, but most of the time they are really basic—a 4-day camping trip with no cell phones, no distractions, and a hard mattress underneath us. Most of the time, they're somewhere in between. It's not really where we're going that matters, I've found. It just matters that we get enough distance from our day-to-day lives to reprioritize each other.

The last time we went on a getaway, we went to a hotel for a long weekend. Some of that time we spent focused on each other cuddled up in fluffy sheets, but most of those 72 hours we spent doing nothing all that special.

I lay in bed until about 10:00 in the morning, waking up whenever I wanted to, *doing whatever I wanted to but in the presence of my partner*. He did the same—rising earlier, taking a long shower, wandering down to the main lobby, moseying into the kitchen to get coffee for himself, sitting on the porch and watching the sunrise. It was perfect. We were around each other with no expectations or obligations whatsoever.

The thing is, when you become a parent, most of your waking hours away from your kids but with your partner are spent in businesslike discussions about schedules, shopping lists, and chores. When you stop and take time to get away, you can choose to forget all that. You can get back to the 2 of you as a partnership but also to the 2 of you as individuals— the people who fell in love with each other in the first place.

I understand that getting away is no easy feat, especially with what's happening around you at the time, especially if taking time to be with your partner feels a little frivolous; it will be the first thing to fall off your priority list anyway. Knowing full well that Murphy's Law applies particularly to good times, I try to think ahead when arranging special moments with my man. You can do the same.

Avoid Overscheduling

The best part about going away with your partner is going and *being*, not *doing*. Even when I know I shouldn't, I have a way of overscheduling myself and others around me. As we plan our getaways, my husband has had to sometimes stop me as I ask about potential timings for sightseeing adventures and activities. Which restaurant looked better to him—the locals' top-rated sushi joint or the pulled pork plate lunch option?

"Relax, baby," I can still hear him saying. "If we do nothing while we're there, it will still be good." All my planning and coordinating are meant to build special memories for my spouse and me, but, in the end, the best moments are almost always spontaneous and unplanned. Sitting on a beach, taking in a sunset, deciding last minute that we want to drive out to a secret cove—these are the moments that stay with me forever. The less planning we do, the less overscheduling we do, usually the better time we have.

Make Sure the Getaway Fits Your Needs

My husband is a really social guy. He's the life of the party. He likes spending time with new people and prefers traveling with other couples. I like traveling most when we travel without other couples, and I'm an introvert with those I don't know well. Sometimes we need different things and its important to be on the same page about these issues. When it's time to relax, we make it a point to have detailed discussions about what we're trying to get out of it all: is this a social adventure with friends or a romantic duo getaway? Is there a way to incorporate both agendas or to plan both types of trips for different times? To make sure we both have our needs met, we set our expectations in advance.

Clear Your Schedule (and Your Kids' Schedules) for When You Return

A few years ago, I was driving home from a trip away with my husband. I planned to take an extra day after our trip to be home with our girls—just me and them—but I forgot one important piece of the return day equation. In my head, I thought only about mindfulness, reminding myself not to be on my phone, doing work, or running errands once I got back to my house. My nanny texted me as I pulled up to the house. She told me she'd planned a playdate at our house that afternoon because she hadn't been sure what time I would return. We could always cancel it, she said, but she bet that my daughter would really love the time with her friend.

I took her up on the offer, figuring it was better not to disrupt previously planned arrangements in the name of making a big fuss about my return. It was a huge mistake. The kids wanted me and me alone. They fought over sharing my lap at the lunch table, they shushed me as I talked to my daughters' friends' mom and tried to catch up with her about camp sign-ups while they played. After about an hour, they each individually looked me in the eyes as if to say, "Please tell these people to go home. I only want to be with you." Lesson learned. In the future, I not only fully cleared my schedule after trips away, I also fully cleared theirs.

Date Nights

You may have heard other people tell you that you should have a date night every week to keep your relationship strong with your partner. In a perfect world, that would be lovely. In the real world, life gets busy. Some weeks, I can barely squeeze in a moment to breathe, much less a date night. Plus, at this point in my marriage, my relationship needs and practical considerations are different than they were in the early days. Sometimes, things seem loud at our house, and all my husband and I want to do is sit at our backyard patio table. We don't need a formal date; we just need time together at our home without the noise of our lives.

Often, when I have alone time with my husband, one of the biggest challenges I face is being present, taking a break from the business manager role I take on in our relationship. It's tempting to make date night an executive meeting about the stuff you and your partner need to accomplish or remember, but make a conscious decision not to let it be. When we put down the checklists and talk about the things that really matter—where we are as a couple, what's going on with our kids (not their activities)—that's when we connect best.

Choose dates that allow you to make memories with your partner, even if planning dates that way means you go out less frequently. When I think back on the moments in my relationship with my husband that have been the most meaningful, they always include at least 2 of these themes: music, good food, a view, or dance. Identifying the activities that have always made you happiest as a couple, that help maintain or get you back into a connected rhythm, will help you plan dates that continue to fan your relationship flame.

Weeknights

Date nights matter, but how about weeknights? In the early days of parenting, it can be impossible to set aside time during the day to relax sans your baby. Your child's feeding needs and your need to prioritize sleep above all else can replace spending unstructured hours with your partner on a consistent basis. As soon as humanly possible, though, think about ways you can shift your schedule to have daily downtime together, whether it be setting an earlier bedtime for your kids or preserving a few moments before you run out the door for work, to talk over coffee.

When my youngest daughter started rebelling against nighttime sleep at around 3 years old, literally telling me she "just was not tired so please get me out of this bed" at 11:00 pm, I limited her naps right away. Yes, I wanted her to have quality sleep onset at the end of her day, but, maybe more importantly, I knew that my relationship with my partner would suffer if we didn't have dedicated time together after 8:30 pm on a consistent basis.

Use weeknight "free time" as an opportunity to be individuals again, but in parallel, without the obligations of parenthood—to remember what it was like to be a couple in your own home before your kids "invaded" it. So what if you don't always use those hours for deep discussions? Sometimes picking up toys off the playroom floor in peaceful silence or sharing funny stories from the day can be just as satisfying.

Your Relationship

If you parent with a partner, taking care of that relationship can feel like one of the least important items on your to-do list, especially when you have multiple little ones in your home. I get it. I've been there.

By the time my husband and I made our decision to make drastic changes in our finances, getting us the freedom we really craved, I was feeling desperate, and my husband was feeling trapped. I'm not sure that he necessarily actually wanted a different life, wife, and kids, but he definitely acted like it, and I definitely felt it. Looking back, he wasn't alone. Both of us really were stuck in a life we felt like we'd almost fallen into that was based on our decision to pursue our individual careers back at the very start of our relationship.

Scott is a smart guy. The kind of smart that can memorize a full list of body parts in a college cadaver lab in one night, the kind of smart that can ace a GRE (Graduate Record Examination) test without a study session. He is the kind of social guy who can wow a crowd with the flash of a smile and a slick dance move. He's loyal, to a fault. He's caring, to the end—the type of person who would give the shirt off his back to a stranger, the roof over his head to a friend in need.

I am a hard worker. The kind of worker bee that grinds day and night, who values perseverance, who works for everything she has. I've never, ever been the smartest or the most clever person in the room, but I've always been the most earnest and the most visionary. I care deeply about my closest relationships, to a fault. I get anxious at a party. I'm social, but only with my inner circle. I'm deeply empathetic and emotionally available when my people are in need, but I can get stingy with my time when I'm feeling overwhelmed myself.

Needless to say, we are different. More different than we realized we were when we were 19 years old and falling in love on a college party dance floor to country line dancing music, lost in each other's strengths, our eyes blind to the ways our personalities stood in stark opposition. Back then, the only concerns we had were biology finals and roommate quarrels—minor blips on the stress chart of life, now that we can see them clearly in hindsight. Life was good and pure, and our differences barely mattered to us.

Years later, with the weight of our finances, our schedules, and our children on our shoulders, those differences felt heavy. Day-to-day, we made it work, but, overall, neither of us felt like we were as strong as we could be. Money was always tight, work was always stressful, our kids seemed to be always having a meltdown. Life took its toll on our relationship. My husband was bored and frustrated as we navigated the very specific requirements of our particularly challenging first child and of our heavy schedules—needs that didn't fit well with a fun-loving, flexible, social existence. I was stuck too; disappointed and resentful about how alone I felt as we worked hard to keep our family boat afloat, the water seeping in through tiny holes in our vessel, carved out by snippy comments and heavy sighs.

Even though we both felt inexplicably lighter when we became significantly less tied to our educational debt, the money didn't solve the damage it had done to our core relationship along the way. That took its own hard work. It took couples counseling. We *still* go to couples counseling, where we keep on working through why we need what we need, how we can approach our yin and yang differences, and what we can do to continue prioritizing each other and each other's desires.

I cannot stress the value of couples counseling enough, even for the strongest relationships. Finding special moments, date nights, is sometimes not enough. If you want to parent as a true team, you've also got to understand the family dynamics of each of your birth families that contribute to the way you interact with each other and with your kids. Figure out what the issues are individually that make it difficult to partner well. Learn from an expert how to really hear each other talk. Discover your deepest needs and your partner's too.

No relationship is perfect. I'm sure people could see my relationship for what it was before I ever could—a rickety rowboat on the high seas—but even the strongest partnerships need work.

Dealing With Generational Expectations and Extended Family Opinions

This chapter deserves a specific comment about dealing with the expectations that others—especially others who are older by a few generations—have for us as we mother and as we co-parent. It's not right, but it is true that we are *still* paving a brand-new path toward greater equity in the home between partners, something most of our grandmothers would have never dreamed of doing, something our mothers fought for but never fully achieved. It may be years and years before we can confidently say we have true partnerships.

That means that those who've lived during less progressive times may have certain, even subconscious, biases about how responsibilities should be divided in your home. They may not fully understand the stresses you face or the direction you're moving toward. They might not even realize the stereotypes they're projecting when they question why or how much *you* work but never do the same for your partner. They may not see how stressful it is when they only ask you about child-rearing, leaving your partner out of important conversations.

When you're faced with less-than-modern thinking, sometimes you just have to ignore it. Sometimes, though, you get the chance to educate about it or to purposefully do your thing despite it, showing your kids a healthier way to co-parent. I'm always adding my husband onto text and email chains about parenting or work plans from extended family. I say things like, "I'll be working that day but he'll be home with the kids. Check with him about the details," or "Oh, he's the one who handles the cooking in our house. If you want it to taste good, you'd better ask him."

If you parent as part of a partnership, it can be easy to let that partnership slide. Taking care of your relationship with your partner and making sure you get real with each other about your co-parenting expectations may be the last thing on your list—something you can't prioritize because you have so many other parts of life pulling on you from all directions. But, take it from me, pushing your partner relationship to the side will eventually catch up with you, keeping you from realizing the dreams you have for your family and for yourself.

One of the most important moments of counseling for my husband and me was when we realized how, in the heat of our struggles and strife, we had stopped dreaming together. Now we have big plans—plans for where we hope our family will be in 5 years, 10 years, 20 years. We're not just sailing around in circles on a rough ocean, we're headed in a specific direction toward a specific destination—a destination we both want to reach *together*. We're truly a team, each with our own individual parts to play as we work together to win at whatever we're working on—including being great parents.

My husband and I don't love each other perfectly or parent together perfectly. We never will. We'll always be as different as the moon and the sun. We're going to continue to sigh and roll our eyes when we're triggered or at our most stressed. At least now we see those relationship infringements for what they are: informational feedback about how we're doing and what we need to adjust to get back to where we want to be—sailing toward an amazing future, steering our family ship together.

Chapter 11

Managing Home and Work Means Not Doing It All

Don't ask what the world needs. Ask what makes you
come alive, and go do it. Because what the world needs
is people who have come alive.

— *Howard Thurman*

I've been watching a lot of Netflix lately. Scratch that. I'm
kind of always watching Netflix. As I sat watching my
weekday dose of it last year, I came across an interesting
show about organizing.

I started watching it because, well, hey, I could use some
tidying tips just like all the other moms I know. It definitely
delivered. I learned a whole new way of folding (basically
fold all your clothes into little rectangles, organize vertically
when possible, and put like shapes or sizes together), but
a few episodes in the message for success with struggling
families was clear: you need less stuff than you think you do,
and you'll be able to enjoy your life more if you only have to
take care of the things you really cherish. Only choose items
in your life that "spark joy."

Like I said, it's a little cheesy, or at least it seems that way
on the surface. Somehow, though, as you watch these families

part ways with their unnecessary clutter and start to truly enjoy their belongings and their spaces, it's almost, dare I say, tear-jerking. Episode after episode you watch people get back to what they intended for their families, for their homes, for their lives. It gets real deep real fast, people.

Of course, that next weekend, I started doing the things I had learned. I went through my house category by category, parting with the excess, neatly folding and arranging. My house *was* definitely cleaner and calmer. It wasn't perfect—with 2 kids under the age of 6 trailing me pulling freshly sorted crayons and toys onto the carpet behind me, it's never going to be—but it was better.

Probably more important than that, though, was the mental process I went through. I learned so much by analyzing, piece by piece, item by item, what I really needed and what was weighing me down—what things I didn't even really care about but just kept picking up and putting back on a shelf over and over again out of routine.

The more I practiced some mindfulness about what sparked joy for me, the more easily I was able to make really good decisions about what I actually wanted my home to be like and to look like (ie, very decluttered).

Plus, the more I looked at my house that way, the more I started to look at my life that way. The more I pondered, the more I started to think about what I go around doing week after week, day after day, that I feel like I have to do—either to keep up with the Joneses or to keep myself overly busy *just because that's what "we moms" do or just because I've never taken the time to think about it.* I started thinking about how sparking joy is usually pretty far down on my priority list (it's high on my list for my kids, but it's relatively low on my list for myself). I started realizing that, not only was it time to clean things out and get more joy in my house, it was also time to declutter my schedule and get more joy in my *home* and with my *family.*

One of the psychologists in my pediatrics clinic taught me a powerful trick to that end because organizing your life according to joy levels is a lot more complicated than deciding to donate a 5-year-old shirt you're done wearing. She asks families she sees in our office to get a monthly calendar and write down all of their obligations—meetings, appointments, big school projects, after-school or weekend activities. Unless it's something they really look forward to all week long, she has them write it all down in red. Then she has them take a blue pen and write down all the activities they do that are for relaxation, for recreation, or for fun.

The results are often shocking to patients as they realize just how much time they spend throughout the week spinning plates. It turns out, the more plates you have to spin, the more work it takes to just keep them all in motion. It's one thing to get my 2 daughters to dance class or to music lessons. It's quite another thing to set 3 alarms a few months ahead so I don't miss the opportunity to sign them up in the first place. No wonder I'm (we're) all stressed to the max. In some ways, we're choosing to be.

Doing Less so You Can Accomplish More

I'm probably never going to perfectly declutter my home while my kids are young. The constant influx of artwork, clothing, and toys almost guarantees that. I can though, along with all the other families I meet, work on a less-is-more mentality. When our physical spaces, our schedules, and our minds are simpler, they allow us to focus more on what really matters, instead of focusing on trying to maintain a bunch of junk. The studies are clear on this when it comes to the workplace, but it's true at home, too: the more scattered you are in your focus, the less productive you are. The more you multitask and overload the system, the less likely you are to do any of your tasks well.

I'm probably never going to be the most organized mom out there. Since perfection is overrated, though, I'm not too worried about getting a Housekeeper of the Year award. To me, getting decluttered isn't just about cleaning up my house (though that is an amazing by-product). The way I declutter or organize might very well change next month—or the next time I watch a Netflix series—anyway. It's more about figuring out what's really important, what really brings joy—in our homes, our schedules, our lives. And, well, who doesn't want a little more of that?

Getting It All Done

There are times when having too much to do means you need to just do less, but, the reality is, not everything can be brushed aside. Households have to run, meals have to be made, clothes have to be washed, checkboxes have to be checked. Even our daily tasks don't have to overwhelm us, though. Efficient working moms use these tricks to get it all done with the least amount of time and stress possible.

They Batch To-dos

Instead of spending all week thinking about what you need to get done to make your life happen, take a chunk of time to make a plan. A half hour should work just fine to organize your day or your week (maybe less once you get really used to this method). Then, set aside another hour or 2 to, in 1 sitting, try to move through as much as possible on your list. If you're still not done once the timer goes off, plan another 2-hour chunk in a few days. Compartmentalizing our to-dos reduces our mental load, allowing us to be more mindful throughout the day.

They Refuse to Equate Chores and Errands With Self-care

Sometimes I take a vacation day, and I spend every minute of it running errands for my family. Usually, by the time

Declutter and "Get Things Done" Department

Use mini whiteboards to visually map out your week. I bought these at the grocery store. They're 6" × 9" whiteboards—1 for my husband and me and 1 for our kids—labeled with each day of the week. Each whiteboard has room to note special events, lessons, meetings, and outings we have planned for the coming week. Some weeks, I look at the whiteboards, and they look crazy with activities. That's OK. If they are, it's a visual reminder that we need to scale back the next week.

Frequently look at your own calendar to analyze where you can simplify. I canceled my daughter's dance class across town because I found a, maybe less than perfect but still totally great, option that required less time on the road. I'm figuring out ways to run at lunch a few days a week when possible. It allows me to clear up my evening time to be with my kids.

Plan for weekend meal planning and grocery shopping. For a long time, I subscribed to weekly meal kit programs. They were especially useful to me when my youngest daughter was just a baby and I had no brain space left to even think about creating wholesome meals for my family. Now, though, my oldest has become quite the kitchen helper. These days, we look through cookbooks or think up meals together on Sundays, take a jog up to the grocery store, and then take a ride share home with everything we need for the week. I have a meal planner outline attached to my fridge with a detachable shopping list I use to keep us on track.

5:00 pm rolls around, I feel tired and grumpy. I often wish I had just gone to work. At the very least, I feel disappointed and wistful about how I used my time. Errands are a necessary evil, but don't get them confused with quality moments alone or with your loved ones. I manage to get most of my checklist items crossed off without lifting a metaphorical finger. You can too (hint: the next 3 tricks are the key to my success).

They Off-load the Tasks That Drive Them Crazy (or That They Don't Do Well)

I'm not always good at cleaning my house. So I hired someone who is, to take care of the number 1 task I don't need or want to do. Hiring a house cleaner reduced my stress, forced me to organize my house the night before she arrived each week, and gave me back my precious time, so I could spend it on more important things, like *anything else.*

I'm also not great at cooking weekday meals other than spaghetti and meatballs or chicken teriyaki out of a freezer bag. I shine when it comes to holiday meal extravaganzas, but my husband is a weekday wiz in the kitchen. Since he and I both know I would probably succumb to takeout every night if he didn't cook consistently (and because we keep working at being parenting teammates), he wears the chef's hat in our home most Mondays through Thursdays.

They Automate

Remember, you are not the only person who can take care of your home, your kids, your bills, or your calendar. The running list of tasks that fills your mind all day long—the appointments you need to make, the dry cleaning you need to take in, the groceries you need to buy—is unhealthy, and it steals away your ability to focus on the here and now. One way to reduce your mental load is to simplify the number of tasks you have, either by getting rid of them or by delegating them to someone else. For the tasks you have to attend to, reduce your time thinking about them by automating.

Thank goodness we live in a modern world where, for a small fee, we can automate almost everything we do. I would wither on the vine if it were not for autopay and internet grocery and household goods delivery services. Diapers, wipes, sippy cups, household items like paper towels, hand soap, and toilet paper—I get them all from online ordering. I do not want to spend my time in a big-box store for basics. Wholesale grocery shopping in person gives me a headache. The regular grocery store is not much better. It's fun to pick out something to add to our family meals or to carefully select a few specialty items when I'm out and about, but using my "me time" to head solo to the store wastes my time. Hauling 2 little people around as I try to shop is also less than ideal.

Instead, I order groceries and household goods every week using online apps and have them delivered to my home within 2 hours. Look for sales or free shipping to help lower the cost. My bills are all on autopay. I shop online for kids' clothes, focusing on quality basics that can be handed down child to child, when possible. I would rather spend a little more money but only have to shop 4 times a year (with some fun, "let's get a special outfit" outings sprinkled in) than pay less per item and have the clothes last less than a month. Another good tip is to shop the clearance racks and pick some items for your child for the next season. This requires a bit of a guessing game on sizing, but a little bigger is usually a good move. I have go-to sites I use regularly for clothing and shoes, so I'm familiar with the sizing and fit—both for my kids and for myself. This is very budget dependent, but, especially if you have multiple kids and they are the same gender, buying quality over quantity makes a big difference.

They Use the Car to Strategically Multitask

The car is your friend. Research shows that multitasking generally decreases our productivity, but, in the car, the same rules don't always apply. The car can be a place to get a lot accomplished in a short period of time.

"I get some of my best work done riding in the passenger seat on family vacations," says working mother Kara, a mom of 2 and a teacher. "I pay bills, research vacation spots, and sign my kids up for swimming lessons. It's like the car creates this special little bubble where creative thinking and strategizing somehow becomes easier."

I'm in full agreement. I think I wrote about half of my first book, *The New Baby Blueprint: Caring for You and Your Little One,* riding shotgun in a car, and most of my blog ideas come to me while I journal on longer trips. Something magical happens when you have your headphones in, your partner is listening to sports radio, and you have no other distractions.

Even when I'm the one driving, I use the car as a mini office. If I'm riding by myself for extended periods, I spend the time in the car listening to podcasts and audiobooks. I love reading paper books, but I just know I would never have the time to get to everything I've had on my "meaning to" list if I relied on my evenings and weekends. That was especially true when I was a new mom. The car was a place where, when I was by myself, I knew I could get a lot done by listening. It still is. Especially when it comes to books in the parenting or self-help sector, audiobooks are the way to go. You can share purchased ones among friends or reserve them from your local library.

As a new parent, I even learned how to pump while driving. If you have a newborn and are nursing, this is one of the most important, time-saving tricks around. I used it with both my children. While parked (safety first!) in my car, I used a hands-free pumping bra to make my outings efficient. Inserting the breast phalanges into the bra and attaching my hands-free pump, I covered myself with a breastfeeding cover, turned that puppy on, and drove wherever I needed to go.

On the way to exercise class, in between meetings, it made my car the perfect pumping station. And it was, obviously, hands-free. I used a cooler pack and disposable cleaning wipes made specifically for breast pump parts for short trips when I didn't have access to a sink. Then I thoroughly washed and sterilized everything once I was home or at work.

When I'm with the kids, who are now older, I try to limit phone calls and work in the car, but I do turn up the stereo and turn on Paul Simon (at a moderate volume) as we cruise along the highway, adding to their music education and to my own enjoyment as we brave the traffic jams together. Playing music in the car doesn't let me get more done, but it does make the time I spend locked in a steel box with my children a unique kind of memory maker opportunity, especially when they start singing along.

Balancing Your Home and Work Lives

What's the most stressful part of being a working mom? Balancing our home and work lives. With 2 jobs—1 at the office and 1 with our children at home—but only 24 hours in a day, it can all get hectic pretty fast. I thought a lot about our collective hectic mindset a few years ago when my family and I made a 60-hour, 780-mile trip down to California and back with a 2- and a 5-year-old in tow.

We were up early on Thanksgiving to catch a 2-hour flight, take a 3.5-hour car ride to my in-laws' house, and eat a lovely meal. Then, we turned around a day and a half later to do it all again. It's one of many November or December trips we've taken with our young kids in the name of tradition and family. And, although I love, love, love my husband's family, and I want my children to be a part of the holiday hubbub, the trip planning (and the beaucoup bucks it costs to make it happen) made us take a second look at our choices.

It also made us take a second look at the trade-offs and benefits of taking a whirlwind attitude toward the holiday months and our lives in general, especially our working parent lives. Something about that Thanksgiving experience sparked a revelation in me about what we all do with our time, especially about what control we have over the parts of our lives that make things feel hectic.

See, here's the deal. When we say we're feeling hectic (especially around the holidays but at plenty of other times throughout the year), we're saying that we've made the choice to make it that way. We're deciding that we agree with living our lives that way. We're saying we *choose* a hectic, stress-filled life.

Now, of course, some things are stressful just because they are. Sometimes a loved one is hurt or ill, sometimes we come across financial difficulties, or a challenging relationship makes life hard. I'm not talking about that kind of stress. I'm talking about hustle and bustle, too many things on our lists, too many commitments, and too many plans kind of stress. I'm talking about self-induced stress.

We've already talked about ways to be more efficient and streamlined in our home lives, but are there ways we can also take better control of our work lives? Are there shifts in perspective that would make your work more enjoyable? Are there practical schedule changes that would get you closer to your real dreams? Just like we have to decide how we want to prioritize on the home front, we also have to decide where we want to place our efforts as we work.

Deciding How Far You Want to Lean In and How Far You Want to Lean Back

I'm not convinced that any working mom can ever have a perfectly balanced work and home life. In my world, the pendulum seems to swing far to one side then back to the other from week to week or month to month, landing somewhere in the middle on average, but never all at once. The way you show up for your life is your business, but, for me, I'm always striving to make decisions about how I spend my days and moments on the basis of priorities. My commitments and efforts when it comes to work are no different.

Thank you from the bottom of my heart to all our working mom predecessors, women who laughed at the idea of balance because they never had the luxury of seeking it. They were ladies who leaned in because they had to. They were pioneers, often fighting discrimination tooth and nail every single day they worked.

On the contrary, in fact. You have to decide when, in your career and in your motherhood stage, you need to take on more or less—not your boss, not the world, not some philosophy—*you*. You have to decide how much you can handle at any one time, what your long-term goals are, where you want to be in a decade or at 80 years old. You have to choose what you want to look back on in your life with contentment and what you may look back on with regret. Maybe this is a season when you need to push, to work hard at work, to sweat it out. Maybe this is a season when you need to hold back, to invest in other parts of you, to focus on mental health or on the health of a loved one.

This life is all about choices. It's a series of trade-offs and benefits. No, you cannot have it all, but you can have more than you ever thought possible if you intentionally choose to live your life on the basis of what's most important to you and according to what you value most.

Asking for Alternative Schedules

I felt like there were about a million roadblocks when I started reprioritizing my life and focusing in on what I really wanted out of it. One of those major barriers was flexibility within my workplace. All of my work partners share the same schedule: 8:30 am to 5:00 pm with a 1-hour midday lunch. We're collegial, but we hold each other accountable when someone excessively blocks his or her own schedule or ducks out early. To pay down our debt, I knew a major component would be creating consistency for my kids and removing potential mishaps for school drop-offs. I had to ask my executive committee for an alternative schedule to make all our puzzle pieces fit together. The shift in hours was minimal—starting 1 hour later and ending 1 hour later than everyone else—but it was still daunting to ask for what I needed to accomplish what felt like a very personal, almost selfish task.

I'm so glad that I did. That tiny change in my work commitments allowed me to be present every single morning for my kids during a year full of transitions and sacrifices. It also allowed me to take other child care providers off of our morning routine completely, saving me stress and money. In the end, a minor schedule alternation was a major win for me.

If you're thinking about asking for an alternative schedule at your work, provide context to your boss about specifically what you want, why you want it, and how it will help you and your company. Let your boss know you can set up formal check-ins to communicate with each other about how it's going and that you are willing to flex as needed. When our employers (or work partners) understand the bonuses of a flexible schedule for us *and* for them, it helps them see the bigger picture and be more flexible themselves.

Saying No: Protecting the Time You Have

If we're going to make major life changes—or just live authentically—sometimes we have to just flat out say no. When it comes to our kids, our jobs, ourselves, we have to actively set boundaries. Believe me, if you keep on giving, others will keep on receiving. Sheryl Sandberg was revolutionary when she talked about leaning in, but if we lean in too far to anything, we're going to *fall in*, victims of our own lack of perspective and mindfulness. That means, at some point, we have to decide what's most important to us. We have to make decisions based on our priorities, not our obligations, or else other people (oftentimes very unintentionally) are going to determine how our minutes and our days are filled.

When my kids look back on their early childhoods, I hope with all my heart they remember the special moments we created decorating Valentine's Day cards on our kitchen table, running through the sprinklers in the summer, and singing all *The Greatest Showman* songs at the top of their lungs in the car. I know they won't remember the toys we buy them or the way their rooms are decorated. Not to be cliché, but it's just the truth: they will remember the times we spend together and the memories we share. If my relationship with myself and with them is my ultimate priority, it means I will have to say no more often to other things that take me away from those priorities. You will have to do the same (so will your partner, if you have one, but this book is not about them, it's about us).

Working From Home With Your Kids Present

Sometimes building flexibility and room for prioritization means shifting *where* we work. If you work from home, it's ideal to have your kids in child care or to have someone present and watching your kids while you work. If you are in a situation where you are the only adult at home during these times, there are a few things you should keep in mind.

- First, set expectations with your kids about the day's activities and what you are doing and why. Ask them for what you need and explain the boundaries.
- Give them age-appropriate distractions; it can be helpful to only allow screen time at these moments to keep their attention longer.

- Have a reward system in place to reinforce good behavior.
- Try to set up calls on days or times your kids aren't there or during normal nap times. Perhaps arrange for grandma or grandpa to stop by right before your call and read a favorite book to your child. Or ensure your calls are with another understanding parent if your kids are present.
- If you expect your kids to interrupt you, proactively let the person on the phone know in advance that it may happen, and explain the situation and how you'll handle it.
- Concentrate on your highest priority work to-dos and those that require the most intense level of attention first. Start your day before your children wake up. This valuable time will be free of interruptions and will have your full attention. If you only have time to work on a few things, make sure they're the ones you really care about or that really need to get done.
- Depending on your schedule, play with your kids early in the day. Kids hate waiting, especially for our attention. Instead of making them more and more frustrated as you make just 1 more conference call, give them the attention they need at the start of the day and get them moving with fresh air and exercise, if possible, early on. Take a walk outside with your kids first thing in the morning when you wake up. When you finally do need to sit down and hammer out a few tasks, they won't be so antsy, and you'll be able to fully concentrate.
- Consider an alternative schedule, especially if you have a partner who is also working from home. Mom may take the 6:00 am to 2:00 pm shift with the kids, then "go to work" in her home office, and dad works 2:00 to 8:00 pm. Or divide up the day. Think about working in 2-hour shifts, switching off with your partner or another caregiver.

- Designate areas of your home for specific tasks, and create visual cues that let your kids know you're off-limits while you're in those spaces. Your garage, the basement, a bedroom—these can all serve as work areas. When you physically separate from your kids and take yourself out of their line of vision, you're less distracted, and your kids are less confused about your accessibility. As the saying goes, "out of sight, out of mind." A red stop sign or a cutout of a hand on your office door is a clear indicator even to young children that work is in session and reinforces that you're not available at the moment.

- Set your kids up for success during important meetings by creating structure. For preschool and elementary children, set up interesting activity centers in their playroom with model clay, craft paper and markers, or books they can interact with while you're away for a short time. For older children, make a list of 10 activities they can do when they feel bored and put it on the refrigerator as a reminder for the times you're off-limits. Use times you're completely off-limits to have them dedicate effort to traditional schoolwork or online learning.

- Plan ahead for food needs. Cut up fruits and vegetables in advance and put them into containers labeled "Meeting Snacks." Make mini quesadillas with protein and veggies, cut them into triangles, and set them out right before your meeting starts. For older kids, set out ingredients for sandwiches or salad before you head into a session with a client or coworker so it's easy for them to put together a snack while you're away.

- Be transparent with your business partners about the fact your kids are in the home with you. The more honest we are about how our home and work lives intersect, the more we normalize that experience for others, and, ultimately, push employers toward considering our whole-person needs as they create policies and culture.

- Above all, give yourself grace. Accept that when you're trying to do 2 jobs simultaneously, you're bound to sometimes be less than perfect at both of them. Take breaks with and without your kids. Definitely don't add even more to your proverbial plate—the errands, the vacuuming, that toothpaste you still need to buy—it can all wait.

enenen

It can be challenging being a working mom and trying to do it all. Have others do more. Figure out—for yourself, not for anyone or anything else—how far you want to lean in or lean back. Live fully alive and awake, moment by moment, mindful that even though we're so much less in control of our lives than we perceive ourselves to be, we do choose exactly how we'll respond to life's challenges and choices, which, ultimately, is what decides where life takes us in the end.

Chapter 12

My Message to Working Moms

*E*ach time I write a blog post, a chapter—even a social media comment—I look back on it carefully, to make sure that it is honest. It's my tendency, just like it's the tendency of almost everyone else I know, to shine things on—making them simpler or more 1-dimensional than they should be, removing the messy parts and sharing only the victories after they've been won. This book was, for me, the ultimate in getting real so that I could help you get real too.

My working mom life is still a work in progress, as I'm sure yours is, as well. Yes, there are tricks and tips that make it easier and less painful, but, ultimately, it's the philosophical aha moments that really move me forward and out of the deepest ruts I find myself stuck in.

A few years ago, I found myself in the deepest rut of my life, but it wasn't my first, and it won't be my last. I wasn't sure what direction my life or some of my most important relationships were going. Those low point moments made me dig down deep and get to what mattered most for me and for my family. I made sacrifices. I made choices. I set my intention and my priorities on what I really cared about, forever changing the way I looked at my career and my working mom life. I aligned my present life with what I wanted my future life to look like, understanding that I couldn't control the future but that I could control the way I prepared for it.

My hope for you as you wade through the ins and outs of motherhood, work, and life is that you find a way to do that same kind of digging, becoming the person you really want to be and living the life you actually want to live. Getting more efficient with our grocery shopping or our commutes make a difference, but those are only minor factors—tiny pieces of a bigger puzzle, pinpoint pixels of a bigger picture.

When will we really be successful as working moms? When we learn how to approach life's choices with a more centered approach based on what matters to us now and what will matter to us when we're older—when the work is done, when our kids are grown, when we've made it to the end of our (hopefully) long lives. That means living by our priorities, taking care of the ones we love most—including ourselves, streamlining our processes, and learning how to approach parenting with a village mentality.

It seems opportunities to prioritize wisely are always on the horizon. My daughter and I are on a girls' trip this weekend, up the coast and across the West Sound on a ferry to Orcas Island, where we'll spend the weekend cozied up in a blanket on a postcard-sized cabin deck playing board games and reading, facing the mountains and the sky, breathing, taking it all in, being quiet. We've been looking forward to it for weeks, talking not about what we'll do but about how we'll be together, just the 2 of us.

She knows and I know it will take hard work and commitment to get there; I'll work at my job to afford it, she'll forgo playdates and maybe more exciting camps to make time for it, my child care reinforcements will work double time caring for my younger child to make it happen. We won't go on other vacations because of it. We'll multitask and delegate all our home tasks and work tasks to allow the brain space for it. I'll miss my other daughter in the process, until I come back to her and hold her sweet hands in mine on our return, reminding her that her own special trip is around the corner.

This weekend is the closest you can get to a life, in perfectly imperfect balance, completely coordinated but requiring work and sacrifice and prioritization.

Taking care of your kids, yourself, and everything else—a pipe dream? Only if we let it be. There is joy waiting for us as we mother, not in spite of our work but alongside it, if we choose relationships, passion, and priorities over obligations and guilt. There is joy in the process, in figuring it out, in deciding what's important and then letting go of what we think we're supposed to do.

Sometimes, things come together faster than we imagine they will when we lay a foundation for success, then let it all unfold. We brought my daughter's bike along with us on vacation, the blue one with the white streamers and the training wheels. She's timid as she rides at first, pedaling slowly, but, like a flash, it all changes. Suddenly, my timid little girl is yelling, "Super speed mode!" as she careens down an island pathway on her bike, shedding her hesitation to ride solo from just a few days prior. She's still got the training wheels on, but she's clattering along as fast as she can, oblivious to the fact she's still in learning mode, not worried at all that she's still not perfectly skilled at this new task.

"I'm building up my stamina, Mama!" she calls back to me, her hair a stream of sunlight as she pumps her little legs and grips the handlebars with all her might, so sure of herself and her newfound strength. My heart is pumping fast too, as we share this moment of connection I will never be able to replicate. Her efforts, I realize, are just like mine as I strive to find my way as a working mom—clanging along loudly with my own training wheels half the time, a hot sweaty mess who could care less how this is looking from the outside as long as, on the inside, I know where I'm going and why I'm working so hard to get there. Remember this the next time you're feeling stuck as you work and mother: growing into our working mom identity, getting wiser, finding balance, leaps and setbacks and all the mucky stuff in-between, it's all part of it. Focus your eyes ahead—on where you're going and on why you're going there—and you'll be sailing toward true joy and contentment before you know it.

Self-care Guides and Resources

Developing Your Priorities Guide

Following are activities we all spend time on, arranged randomly:

Work
Homemaking
Kids
Hobbies and sports
Partner

Appearance
Friendships
Exercise and stress reduction
Travel and experiences

STEP 1. Rank these activities in order based on what you, in an ideal world, would spend the most time on or doing. Rank them as a private, honest list, not based on how you think other people would want you to rank them or how you think you should rank them.

IDEAL LIST

_____

_____

_____

_____

_____

_____

_____

_____

_____

STEP 2. Rank the activities based on what you actually spend time on throughout the week or month.

REALITY LIST

_____

_____

_____

_____

_____

_____

_____

_____

STEP 3. Compare your first list (your Ideal List) with your second list (your Reality List). How do they match up?

IDEAL	REALITY

STEP 4. Use the top 3 items on your Ideal List to help you determine a self-care ritual. What 3 activities could you incorporate into your week to honor the priorities you want to define your life?

1. _____

2. _____

3. _____

STEP 5. Use the bottom 3 items on your Ideal List to help you determine what tasks you need to delegate or minimize effort around. What 3 chores could you remove from your to-do list or give to someone else?

1. _____

2. _____

3. _____

Goal-Setting Guide

Setting goals based on our ideal life versus our current life opens our mind to possibilities we may not otherwise consider.

STEP 1. Visualize your well-prioritized life.
Close your eyes and let your mind wander. Visualize yourself with your priorities in-line, living your most authentic life. Where are you? What are you wearing? What does it smell like around you? What colors do you see? Where are you going? Think about who you're with and what you're doing. Notice what's around you.

Consider your Ideal List from the last exercise. Based on those priorities, list your biggest goals. Think big. Forget about what your life looks like now (your Reality List) as you do this exercise and instead think about what you want it to look like.

EXAMPLE: I will be financially secure.

1. _____

2. _____

3. _____

4. _____

5. _____

STEP 2. Pick 1 dream to focus on. Now, write 3 goals to get to that dream. Make sure they're SMART—specific, measurable, attainable, realistic, and time bound.

Specific

Make sure you have a concrete goal in mind. "I want to feel better about myself" is not a goal. It's a great reflection. It's a starting place, but it's just too ambiguous. There is no way to tell if you've actually achieved your goal once you get there.

Measurable

Measurable goals have an outcome you can assess after a certain amount of time to determine your level of progress. That way, you know when you've met your goal and can set a new goal.

Attainable

If you set a goal that is too far out of reach, the chances of you reaching that goal are pretty slim. Instead, set a goal that is possible to reach. For example, an unattainable goal for me would be, "I will be a marathon runner next month." Instead, "I will complete a 10-km run in 3 months," is more likely.

Realistic

Realistic goals are goals that are not based in fantasy. Instead, they are possible to achieve, even if it takes multiple, painful steps to get there.

Time Bound

Even with self-care goals, time is an important element. For example, "My goal is to write a children's book by 1 year from now. I'll do step x by 1 month from now, step y by 2 months from now, and step z by 3 months from now to work toward that goal."

EXAMPLE: In 3 years, I will have no consumer or student loan debt.

1. _____

2. _____

3. _____

STEP 3. Set 3 mini goals to achieve that larger goal. Make sure the mini goals are positive—things you will do, not things you won't do.

EXAMPLE: I will bring my lunch from home every day to work (not "I won't eat out at lunch").

Go big if you can, but make sure the goals are very specific here.

EXAMPLE: I will reduce my child care costs by 50%.

1. _____

2. _____

3. _____

STEP 4. Choose 1 goal to focus on first.

Write out all the factors you'll need to consider to make that goal happen. This is where you want to deep dive on potential pitfalls that could trip you up or think outside the box about how you might make it happen. Once you've worked out the details to get to that goal and have started to make a change, move onto the next goal, still within that dream.

PITFALLS	GOAL

Partner Care Planning Guide

List 4 activities you and your partner each like to do individually.

YOU

_____

_____

_____

_____

PARTNER

_____

_____

_____

_____

List 4 experience activities you and your partner could do locally together (think beyond dinner and a movie—for example, concerts, hikes).

_____

_____

_____

_____

List 4 bigger experience activities you and your partner could do together (trips, events).

_____

_____

_____

_____

POTENTIAL CHILD CARE OPTIONS

_____

_____

_____

_____

_____

_____

_____

POTENTIAL BARRIERS

_____

_____

_____

_____

_____

_____

Index